TOGETHER, ALONE

SOUTHWESTERN WRITERS COLLECTION SERIES
The Wittliff Collections at Texas State University–San Marcos
Steven L. Davis, Editor

Together, Alone

A MEMOIR OF MARRIAGE AND PLACE

Susan Wittig Albert

UNIVERSITY OF TEXAS PRESS

Austin

The Southwestern Writers Collection Series originates from the Wittliff Collections, a repository of literature, film, music, and southwestern and Mexican photography established at Texas State University–San Marcos.

Requests for permission to reproduce material from this work should be sent to:
  Permissions
  University of Texas Press
  P.O. Box 7819
  Austin, TX 78713-7819
  www.utexas.edu/utpress/about/bpermission.html

♾ The paper used in this book meets the minimum requirements of
ANSI/NISO Z39.48-1992 (R1997) (Permanence of Paper).

LIBRARY OF CONGRESS CATALOGING-IN-PUBLICATION DATA
Albert, Susan Wittig.
Together, alone : a memoir of marriage and place / Susan Wittig Albert. —
1st ed.
    p.   cm. — (Southwestern writers collection series)
ISBN 978-0-292-71970-5 (cloth : alk. paper)
1. Albert, Susan Wittig. 2. Authors, American—20th century—Biography.
3. Married women—United States—Biography. I. Title.
PS3551.L2637Z46 2009
813'.54—dc22
[B]   2009010632

For Bill Albert,
who makes all journeys possible;
for Bob Goodfellow, always a friend;
and for Father Francis Kelly Nemeck,
a guide along the way.

Loyalty to place arises . . . from our need to be at home on the earth. We marry ourselves to the creation by knowing and cherishing a particular place, just as we join ourselves to the human family by marrying a particular man or woman.

SCOTT RUSSELL SANDERS, *STAYING PUT: MAKING A HOME IN A RESTLESS WORLD*

What marriage offers—and what fidelity is meant to protect—is the possibility that what we have chosen and what we desire are the same.

WENDELL BERRY, *THE UNSETTLING OF AMERICA*

CONTENTS

Documenting a Life

It is our inward journey that leads us through time—forward or back, seldom in a straight line, most often spiraling. Each of us is moving, changing. . . . As we discover, we remember; remembering, we discover.

EUDORA WELTY, *ONE WRITER'S BEGINNINGS*

THIS MEMOIR LOOKS BACK over twenty-some years of life experience. It encompasses times of joyous discovery and hopeful anticipation, times of loss and sadness and anger. But memory is a shape-shifter and a deceiver, capable of altering our view of all past realities into a cleverly crafted perception that fits with our present view of self-in-world. Memory conceals, invents, flatters. Memory makes mythology. You can't trust memory to tell the truth. I can't, anyway.

What made this memoir possible was not memory, that notoriously unreliable beast, but my habit of keeping a daily journal, or at least a daily diary, when there wasn't time for serious, introspective writing. I've held on to these notebooks and computer files, resisting the occasional temptation, in a fit of housekeeping tidiness, to chuck the whole lot of them into the rubbish. There's certainly a lot of trash in those pages—whines, complaints, angry rants, mindless raves, the effluvium of life caught on the fly. But there's good stuff there, too. People and events I've forgotten, feelings I've hidden, patterns I couldn't see then but that would emerge with time, details that slipped through the cracks of the floor of my mind and into the cellar where unremembered things lie, dark, dust-covered, silent.

The journal has been my traveling companion as I've backtracked along the trail of the last couple of decades. Because it's there to read and refer to, I've had to deal only with the distortions of the present point of view (that is, the present of the journal, in whatever year it was written), rather than the inevitable distortions I'd see if I looked into the past through the unreliable mirrors of memory. I can't lay claim to absolute truth, of course, any more than you can, when you tell your own story. But I will lay claim to the relative truths of my perceptions, while I candidly admit to their selectivity, slanting, inexactness, and incompleteness.

I've journaled since I was in graduate school at Berkeley in the late 1960s. Oh, those years, chaotic, cataclysmic, incoherent—a single mother with three young kids, Peace Park up the hill, Haight-Ashbury across the Bay, a dissertation in the typewriter. These were the years of the Flower Children and antiwar protests and Kent State, and all that tumultuous energy lives still in my journal. Sometimes I wrote regularly, sometimes intermittently, but more regularly and more obsessively as the years went along. Each year, on my birthday, I made it a practice to reread and annotate what I wrote during the previous year; every few years, I'd pick a period to revisit and spend a day or so rereading several years' worth of journals. I have never failed to be astonished, or enlightened, or amused, or perturbed, or embarrassed. And I have never failed to learn something new about myself, something I didn't already know, or something I knew once and had forgotten.

As I wrote this memoir, I read through a cache of sixteen thick handwritten notebooks and more than five hundred single-spaced pages of computer print-out, covering the years between 1985 and 2006. I've included some of the entries in this memoir—not because they are especially well written or describe some momentous event, but because they are typical in their every-daily-ness. And because they help to frame my story in the context of what really happened.

The journal has lived through several incarnations, from notebook to computer and now (at least in part) to cyberspace. I first kept my blog, Lifescapes, on my Web site, then moved to first one blog host and then another, looking for the right home. I'm now settled at www.susanalbert.typepad.com/lifescapes. There, you'll meet my public self, the self I like to present to the world. For the private self, you'd have to dig into the notebooks I still keep.

Together, these public and private explorations are as reliable a record of my past lives and invented selves as I am ever likely to have.

TOGETHER, ALONE

CHAPTER ONE

Meadow Knoll

Getting Here, Alone Together

'Tis a gift to be simple, 'tis a gift to be free.
'Tis a gift to come down where you want to be,
And when we find ourselves in the place just right
'Twill be in the valley of love and delight.

"SIMPLE GIFTS," TRADITIONAL SHAKER HYMN

July 7, 1986. Austin, Bill's house. Early morning sunshine, and already hot, in the 80s. The grapes are ripe. I take a large basket outside and in twenty-five minutes have picked six pounds of ripe grapes, juicy, sweet-tart, purple. The vines are so heavy they have broken some of the lathes of the trellis. The mockingbird scolds me as I pick—these are his grapes—and dive-bombs the cats. They are watching me from the porch, pleased to have my company. Inside, in the kitchen, it's still cool. I wash and pick the grapes over, delighting in their roundness, their silvery sheen, and now they are cooking into juice.

February 27, 1987. Back from our long trip through the Northwest. I'm glad not to be on the road (living 24-7 in Grace has its stresses), and I'm grateful to have a nice house to come home to, even if it is piled high with stuff at the moment. But it's hard to come home to the city, and Austin is a very large city. How had I forgotten that? Back in the land of Yuppies and IBM execs, I feel utterly alien. I hate the traffic, the blaring billboards, the careless ugliness of the landscape, the politics, and the Texas mega-hype that infects everything. I need a quieter landscape where things don't shout so.

IT WAS LATE APRIL 1987, when Bill and I parked Amazing Grace at the top of the knoll where the land sloped down to the clear creek that bordered the five acres of Texas Hill Country that Bill had bought some thirteen years before. Meadow Knoll, we were calling it. We spent the warm, bright afternoon walking through the green willows and the cattail marsh and up the creek to the lake, where we sat on the grass under arching live oaks, watching and listening. A great blue heron waded on yellow stilts in the frog-rich shallows while a kingfisher, master diver, sliced cleanly through air and water in pursuit of lunch and an American kestrel hovered over a clump of grass before swooping onto its prey—mouse? grasshopper? nestling? Flocks of barn swallows banked and turned in synchronized flight, as a male red-wing blackbird trilled his brash, territorial *oak-a-le-e-e: Outta here! This is my patch of marsh!*

In the evening, we walked back through the cooling wind to Amazing Grace, our eight-by-fifteen-foot orange-and-white recreational vehicle. I made soup on the propane stove and sandwiches from what I found in the refrigerator that operated on either propane or electricity, and we took our food outdoors to eat while we watched the red-orange sun splash like a globe of lava into puddles of red-and-purple clouds beyond the trees.

As dusk fell across the land, we listened to the low, breathy *who-whoo-whoo* of a great horned owl calling from the edge of the woods, like someone blowing over the top of a bottle, and the leaf-rustling blunders of an armadillo under the oak trees. And then, because we were far from the lights of Austin, the sky became very, very dark, studded with thousands of very, very bright stars, while the Big Dipper ladled out the Milky Way. After a long time, we went inside and lay in our double bunk, listening to the sound of the wind brushing the evergreen junipers, the frogsong along the creek, the querulous croak of a green heron. I stayed awake, watching the sky through the window, and in a little while, I saw a star fall like a blazing gift.

We didn't know it yet, but we had come home.

IN THE SEVEN MONTHS since Bill and I married, Amazing Grace had been our home-on-the-road. Grace had lived a hard life before I bought her, and she needed patient attention. Twelve years old, she had a tendency to occasional mechanical misadventures and apparent givings-up-of-the-ghost that Bill, to my utter amazement, always managed to repair. (We joked that I married him to manage Grace, whose automotive peculiarities were beyond my rudimentary mechanical skills.) Wearing a canoe lashed like a jaunty hat up-top, Grace took us from central Texas to the northern tip of Nova Scotia and back again on our September–October honeymoon. Later, in January and February, she took us home-hunting from Texas to California (oh, awesome Yosemite buried in deep snow, coyotes calling out the moon in the nearly empty campground), north to rainy Oregon and wintry Washington and back through Idaho, Montana, and Colorado.

As we drove across the mountains and plains, we talked long and seriously about the kind of life we wanted to make together, the sort of place we wanted to live. We would drive through a valley and try to imagine what it would be like to live there, perched on the side of that mountain, surrounded by forest. Or there, beside that tumbling, rocky stream, or in that green oasis of cottonwood trees, or on the red rim of that desert, or in the countless small towns we passed through along the way.

And often, as encouragement to Grace, when she lumbered up a hill or along a featureless stretch of highway, we sang her favorite song, sang all the verses, always ending with the one we liked best: "Through many dangers, toils and snares, we have already come. T'was Grace that brought us safe thus far, and Grace will take us home."

And she had. But not to a desert or a mountain. To the small, unspectacular patch of land in the Texas Hill Country that Bill already owned, which had seemed too commonplace, too ordinary for consideration.

"And Grace will take us home."

BILL ALBERT AND I were married on a crisp, sunny fall equinox in 1986. After the outdoor ceremony at Austin's Zilker Botanical Garden, everyone came to our house to share the wedding buffet we had prepared—baked ham and my specialty potato salad and quiche and an elegant carrot cake baked by my daughter Robin. My grown-up children were there, Bobby and Robin and Michael, and my brother John Webber and his family and Bill's brother John Albert and his family and Mom and Dad Albert, and a flock of friends, his and mine. And then they all hugged us and wished us well and went away and Bill and I were alone.

Well, almost. There was Grace, of course. And OJ and Eureka! and PK, the cats. But basically, and from now on, there would be just the two of us.

This life was to be very different from the life I had been living. The previous year, in my mid-forties, I had traded my secure position as vice president and tenured English professor at Southwest Texas State (now Texas State University) for a tenuous future as a fiction writer. At the time, tenured women and women in university administration were an academic minority (may still be, for all I know), and my colleagues and friends thought I was crazy, giving it all up—or throwing it away, depending on your point of view. Some of them said so to my face; others whispered it behind my back.

Crazy? Probably. In those days, women who were determined (and lucky) enough to get as far as I had usually kept right on going. And if it wasn't crazy, it was undeniably outrageous, a shocking, brazen, ungrateful thumbing-my-nose at the system that had nurtured and groomed and promoted me. But I hadn't gotten where I had by following the rules, had I? If I'd listened to one of my graduate professors at the UC Berkeley, I'd be teaching high school English— that's what Dr. Oliver suggested I do, when he learned that I would be thirty-two by the time I earned my PhD. In his book, that was far too late to begin an academic career, especially for a woman.

Anyway, I had learned what I set out to learn and achieved enough to know that I could have the rest if I wanted to work for it. Yes, I was retiring early from the battlefield. I was leaving major wars unfought, but that would be true whenever I left, wouldn't it? There would always be one more battle, one more curriculum project, one more round of budgets and tenure and promotion. I was divorced and my children were grown and independent, more or less, with families of their own. If I was ever going to do anything different with my life, turn it in any new direction, now was the time.

And that's what I did, through a stroke of amazing, inexplicable, and, still to this day, unbelievable luck. As if it were an unexplored continent awaiting discovery, I happened upon a new life that suited me, and for which I was suited. Before I began my undergraduate work at the University of Illinois in the early 60s, when my children were babies and I was still a full-time wife and mom, I had written and published magazine fiction for children and young adults. When I began to think of ways to earn a living outside the university, I decided to try this kind of writing again, but book-length, rather than short stuff. I studied the market, wrote three sample chapters and a plot outline of a book called *Summer Breezes*, and (by some magic I still don't understand) sold it—without an agent—to the editor of a young adult mass market series published by Bantam Starfire. (Years later, I was astonished to receive a copy of that little book in the mail, translated into a language I didn't even recognize. Who knew?)

In the year I left the university, I wrote and sold several more novels for young adults. This was "work for hire," and I'd never make a name for myself or amass a fortune doing it. But I didn't care. I'd already earned my share of recognition, and anonymity, even invisibility, held a certain appeal. The writing brought me enough to live on, and that was all I asked. Six or seven years later, after I began writing the books I really wanted to write, under my real name, I would come to see that these short novels had provided a useful apprenticeship in the craft and business of fiction. But when I began (or rather, began again, since I had started writing fiction some twenty-odd years before), the writing was always and only a job, a means to an end: to bring my work home.

And this was vitally important to me, for working at home had become one of the major goals of my new life. When I worked at the university, I was away from home, on the campus, days and evenings and even weekends. In fact, some of us regarded the clock as a badge of honor. Putting long hours into the job was an investment, a demonstration of your commitment, especially if you were a woman. It was how you got ahead in a highly competitive organization. But, in fact, I preferred this way of ordering my life. Burying myself in books and teaching and administrative duties was a way of escaping from some troublesome truths I wasn't able (or didn't want) to acknowledge. This was not a healthy state of affairs, but for a long while—ten years, twelve—that didn't matter.

Then, unexpectedly and quite urgently, it *did* matter. I wanted to work at home, where I was not at someone else's beck and call. I wanted to plan my own work, work to my own plan, without interruption, without distraction. Wanted to work in the solitude of my own space, my own place. Wanted to work alone, rather than in a community of fellow workers, where I was continually on call for other people's demands and emergencies. My own emergencies were demanding enough.

And there were other, compelling wants. I wanted time. Time to read something other than the narrowly focused, purpose-driven academic reading I'd done since graduate school. Time to stumble over new books, amble after new interests. Time to explore my self, to learn who I was, in a creative and purpose*less* way, because setting a purpose would construct perimeters around what I was to learn, who I was to be. Time to garden, to quilt, to knit, to walk in the woods, to learn the names of birds and plants, to be with my grown-up children, to nap with my cats.

But more than any of this, I wanted to live in the country, away from cities, towns, people. Although I'd spent most of my adult life in cities, the country was in my heart, in my bones. My mother grew up on a farm near Milan, Missouri, in the nineteen-teens and -twenties. She took us there for summer visits, dragging my younger brother John and me and all our gear onto the train for the twelve-hour trip across the prairies of Illinois and Missouri.

When I was four, we moved to a farm owned by Raleigh Dawson, near State Line, Indiana. We'd been living in Maywood, Illinois, in the middle years of World War II, and Dad was working at a munitions plant in neighboring Oak Park. He read about the tenant farmer job in the Help Wanted section of a Chicago newspaper. To please my mother, I think, or as a demonstration to her that he actually intended to stop drinking (he didn't), he applied for the job.

Everything about the farm fascinated me: the sunny meadows and mysterious woods, the outdoor privy, the red-painted iron water pump, the kerosene lamps with glass chimneys that my mother washed and rinsed with vinegar in an enameled dishpan. I adored the raucous white geese, the Rhode Island Red hens that pecked my hands when I reached into their nests for eggs, and Daisy, the docile, doe-eyed brown cow. Loved helping my mother do laundry in a gasoline-powered washing machine with a wooden wringer that I was forbidden to touch lest it snatch my fingers. Loved watching Dad milk Daisy, my happiest memory of a man who struggled through all the years of his life with alcoholism and other unknowable demons. Loved watching Mom separate the cream from Daisy's fresh milk, loved turning the wooden handle on the churn until the butter thickened and Mom took over the churn to finish the task. Loved patting the butter into balls with a wooden paddle and forming them with the round butter press that my grandfather's father, James King Franklin, had carved of maple before my grandfather was born. The press left the imprint of a flower on the lovely golden butter. It left an imprint on me, too, on my spirit. I still have the press and the churn, dear possessions.

The farm job had belonged to a man who had gone to fight in the war. When he returned from overseas, he took back the job and the farmhouse and the chickens and geese and Daisy the cow. To my utter sorrow, we moved to town, to Danville, Illinois, where I began grade school. But two town moves and several jobs later (my father's drinking did not endear him to employers), we were back in the country, living on a tenant farm near Bismarck, Illinois, in a landscape of steamy cornfields and fecund river bottoms and wide skies loud with the glorious hurrahs of wild birds.

I was home again. I didn't need playmates, which was a good thing because there weren't many, and my brother had his own interests to pursue. I loved being alone. I climbed the catalpa tree outside my bedroom window and read library books while I listened to Harry Caray and Joe Garagiola call the St. Louis

Cardinals play-by-play. I rambled through the woods and rode my bike for miles along country lanes—no thought of danger for a young girl exploring on her own in those innocent days. I dug potatoes and picked peas in my mother's garden and hoed vagrant corn out of orderly rows of beans in fields so big I couldn't see the end of the row. I was paid ten cents an hour, enough to buy the occasional bottle of Evening in Paris perfume and red polish for my toenails (I was forbidden to wear it on my fingernails). I fished for bluegills and crappies and catfish—it took courage to dare those barbed catfish!—in the muddy North Fork of the Vermilion River, under a rusty iron bridge. That bridge was destroyed by a flood long ago, but I can still hear its metallic rattle-and-clank in my dreams.

And I spent weeks every summer on Grandma and Grandpa Franklin's Missouri farm. Its garden and chickens and cows and pigs had fed my mother's family well, and its woodlots had kept them warm during the lean years of the Depression. Grandma and Grandpa lived that way long into the 1950s, independent, self-sustaining, needing little beyond what they could produce for themselves. I remember—this must have been 1945 or '46—riding with Grandpa in his wagon, its wooden wheels rimmed with iron, sitting high on the seat behind his team of muscular, heavy-hoofed brown horses, manes and tails brushed and shining, bodies ripe with rich sweat and studded with horseflies, which Grandpa expertly flicked away with the tip of his whip. We were on our way to trade Grandma's butter and eggs for flour and sugar and coffee at the Milan general store on the town square.

I felt a deep admiration for my grandfather, whose strength was dignified by decades of hard, physical work and who guided those huge horses with the lightest touch of the reins. This was just after the close of the war, and tractors were rapidly replacing horses and mules on farms all across the country. But not on my grandfather's farm. His horses pulled the wagon, pulled the wooden sledge that hauled water from the creek or rocks for the road, pulled the plow that turned the soil in my grandmother's garden, pulled the mowing machine that cut the hay, leaving it in orderly windrows to cure. There may come a day, perhaps, when we will wish for horses and horse-drawn implements and the skill to use them.

I felt the same admiration for my grandmother, who made perfect biscuits without a recipe, without even a measuring cup, mixing flour and butter and milk in a white enamel basin, mixing the dough with her hands, flattening it with a hand-carved rolling pin, and cutting out circles with a jelly glass. She baked the biscuits in a wood-fueled cookstove and served them with redeye gravy and smoked ham from their own pigs. Breakfast always included fried eggs, fried potatoes, fried tomatoes and onions, Cream of Wheat, and the last piece of yesterday's pie, saved for Grandpa. Noontime dinner was another hot meal: chicken or pork, sometimes beef; potatoes mashed or fried; vegetables from the garden in season or from the gleaming blue Ball jars with zinc lids lined up on sagging shelves in the fruit cellar; pies made of fresh or canned fruits; more biscuits, with Grandma's jams and jellies. Supper was cold, assembled from what was left of noon's dinner, sometimes simply biscuits and milk.

Electricity came to the farm in the late 1940s, and Grandma bought a refrigerator first and then a washing machine. The refrigerator took the place of the springhouse, that cool and mysterious place covered with orange-blooming trumpet vines, with a cold water spring that bubbled up under a wooden box in the back corner. Grandma kept milk and butter and eggs there, always cool, even in the hottest summers.

The electric washing machine replaced the washboard and hand wringer and must have marked a major turning point in Grandma's life. Grandpa wore bib overalls. Wet, they were heavy enough to sag the clothesline that ran across the backyard. Eventually, a gas stove replaced the kitchen range, and cakes (easier to bake in the even-tempered gas oven) began to appear as often as pies. The crank phone on the kitchen wall came down and was replaced by a black handset in the parlor, and the party line became a private line, much to Grandma's disgust. She always felt more connected when she could ring up Sylvia Search, who lived a half-mile down the road, by simply cranking two longs and a short, and if Mrs. Glidewell wanted to talk too, why, she was perfectly welcome. The party line gone, Grandma had to dial o for the Milan switchboard operator, who would then put through her call to the Searches. "Long way around Robinson's barn," she'd say, and frown. And since the line was private, so was the call. Mrs. Glidewell had to wait.

My dream, when I was a girl, was to live as my grandparents lived: in a small white house on a low green hill, with woods and fields and streams holding me in a sweet, enduring embrace through summer sun and winter blizzards, easy times and hard. I didn't try to calculate how this would be paid for, or imagine the kind of living I might earn out there, away from the city. I only thought of being in such a place, and being alone.

But as I grew up, my fondness for country places was overtaken by a desire to get somewhere, make something of myself. I went to a very small high school, in Bismarck, Illinois, and graduated in a class of forty-two students. I married Bob in 1958, the day after graduation, got pregnant immediately, and then again, and again, three children in four years. They were good years, and a good husband and children, and I loved them all and was happy, but time for myself, time alone—well, there wasn't any of it. Every hour of every day belonged to the family. It was the natural order of things, or so it seemed.

And then, in 1963, I found Betty Friedan's *The Feminine Mystique* in our small local library. (I wonder now what this incendiary book was doing there.) I read it, and the world turned upside down. And then upside down again, when I enrolled later that year at the University of Illinois. And then again, when I earned a graduate fellowship and took the family off to the University of California at Berkeley, where I earned a PhD in English. My first teaching position, in 1972, was at the University of Texas at Austin; my first full-time administrative position was at Newcomb College of Tulane University in New Orleans in 1979, and the second at Southwest Texas State in San Marcos in 1981.

All these were good years, certainly, and there were many achievements, although a certain part of myself always felt vaguely resentful when she looked at the day's schedule, the week's calendar, and saw that—once again, just as it had been when the children were small—every hour of every day belonged to someone else. I was trading personal time for professional achievement, although I didn't put it to myself in those terms. I suppose I didn't dare. If I had articulated it that clearly, I might have had to make a change.

A great deal of what I was able to accomplish in those years came about because I was free to move. "Must be willing to relocate" was a common mantra of the career culture in the 1960s and 70s. To stay mobile and to be upwardly mobile, I couldn't afford attachments. Connections to a person, to a place, would limit the possibilities, tie me down, anchor me. A woman who was free to move on, move up, was ready for success. I had children, yes, but (by that time) no husband, and the children could relocate with me. And later, I had a husband who was willing to live in one city while I lived in another—until that marriage broke up, and I was once again unattached.

I'm not the only one who cultivated nonattachment, of course. Americans, as Wayne Fields has suggested, are "proudly-untethered." We are "more a people of highways than of places," a mobile people, swept along on the many westering waves of exploration that have reshaped this continent since the first Old World pilgrims set foot on the New. My people belonged to that footloose tribe. On my mother's side, my great-great-great-grandfather Conrad Franklin drove a covered wagon west from Mercer County, Kentucky, to Sullivan County, Missouri, in 1849, in the company of his sons and daughters and their families. On my father's side, my great-grandmother Jane Jackson Turnell, an English housemaid, up sticks and sailed to America in 1870 with her husband (a brewer's dray-man) and two small children. Another part of the same family emigrated from Germany about the time of the American Revolution. My family tree has lots of limbs and branches, but scarcely any roots.

For me, and for many other women and men, mobility was an essential part of my education, and after that, of my professional development. Just as importantly, it was essential to my personal development. I learned something new in every new place—Berkeley, Austin, New Orleans—and all the places and people in between helped me see who I was, who else I might be. If I had been a homebody, stayed put on familiar ground, lived for keeps in a single place, how could I have learned these things about myself, about others, about the world?

I remember reading John Berryman's poem "Roots" and feeling the slash-ing truth of his line, "exile is in our time like blood." It was so. To me and many others, exile was heart's blood, mind's blood, life's blood, stronger than any blood ties to people or place. And necessary. Exile gave me the freedom to look back over my shoulder and dislike what I saw. During this robust, roaming, learning, liberating period of my life, I remembered the Midwest of the 1950s with distaste: the parochialism of our neighbors and yes, of my family, too; the prejudice, the narrow-minded ignorance; the insistence on being always mor-ally and religiously and politically right. I understood Carol Kennicott, the pro-tagonist of Sinclair Lewis' 1920 novel *Main Street*, who was oppressed by the numbing conformity, the dull speech, the rigid requirements of respectability. And I certainly agreed with her that dishwashing wasn't enough to satisfy all women.

And yet, and yet. As time went on, I began to be aware of an increasing sense of rootlessness and placelessness, a feeling that the price I paid for exile, however necessary, was a certain homelessness. I belonged nowhere. Partly, this feeling came from spending so much of my time in books about a past (Medi-eval and Renaissance England) that was so entirely foreign to my experience, so utterly other than the present. Partly, it was due to my commitment to mobil-ity, to my fear of becoming attached, and to a sense that there was always some other *where* that might be more attractive, more professionally rewarding, more interesting than the *here*.

Whatever the cause, by the time I was in my early forties, I began to be aware of my rootlessness and feel a new kind of wanting, something entirely un-expected, compelling, disturbing. The rural landscapes of my childhood, which seemed more real and rooted than the abstract ideas and academic politics of my adulthood, now called out urgently. Those old desires began to find a voice, and I began to try to imagine what it would be like to stop moving around and settle somewhere, some *where* that looked and felt like . . . well, like home.

At first, I dismissed this as mere sentiment, a belated homesickness, a midlife nostalgia. But what is sentiment but an impulse of the heart, a sighed *yes, yes*? Yes, this is mine, me, where I belong. Yes, this is who I am. And what is homesickness but a desire to be at home, to be in place, to dwell in the *here* from whence we came?

Before long, my dreams and daytime imaginings were full of remembered landscapes, and I began to think of having a small place in the country with chickens, a garden, fruit trees. I could drive back and forth to the university—many people did, and it satisfied them. But that wasn't what I wanted. I couldn't really *live* in the country, in a full, whole-hearted way, if I had to divide my day between home and work. In order to have the kind of life I wanted, I had to leave the life I had. And on the day I walked out of the university, I felt astonishingly, astoundingly free—as free as those wild birds—and I could sing my own glorious hurrah. It was only a step, but it was the first, and it was necessary.

I MET BILL ALBERT some months after I left the university. A statistician and computer systems analyst with a degree in Industrial Management, Bill had worked at a variety of positions in state government and the software industry, jobs with ever increasing responsibilities, heavier workloads, greater conflicts, and less and less satisfaction. When I told him my leaving story, he replied that he, too, was at the leaving point.

It was the first of many discoveries of the things we had in common. Bill had done a great deal of technical and analytical writing: software documentation and reports for the Governor's Office of Equal Employment Opportunity, the Committee on Aging, and the Bureau of Indian Affairs. We thought we might be able to write together (an idea that occurred when he helped me solve a plot puzzle in a Nancy Drew mystery I was writing). An amateur historian and archaeologist, he was deeply interested in the cultural impacts of changing technologies. He was an adventurer, too: a photographer, a pilot, a skin diver, a spelunker, a world traveler. A skilled woodworker, he collected and restored antique hand tools, not for the pleasure of acquisition, not for display, but for use.

All this was very nice. But there was more, and better. Like me, he wanted to find ways to work at home. In 1974, he had acquired five acres in the Hill Country, an hour's drive northwest of Austin. The little place had a creek, a knoll, a meadow, and a wood, within walking distance of a small, man-made lake. It was located on a gravel track some two miles off an unpaved county road, and its isolation and remoteness appealed to him. He built a tiny cabin and spent weekends there, learning the seasons of the land, learning how to be at home there, learning how to be alone.

Shared philosophies, a mutual interest in writing, a common willingness to build a life away from the distractions of the city, an increasingly intense personal attraction—well, you can see where this was going. My chief reservation was getting enough time to myself; I had lived alone, or mostly so, for five years, and the solitary hours were very sweet. Bill had the same reservation; he had lived alone for most of his adult life, and he was uneasy about surrendering the freedom that comes with being responsible for (and to) only the self. How we were going to negotiate this issue wasn't clear.

A lot of other things weren't clear, either. The writing jobs I'd been lucky enough to get—how long would they keep coming? Without the writing, what would we do to make money? I had already given up my job; should he hold onto his? Where would we live? What would our lives be like?

We didn't know the answers to any of these questions. We only knew that whatever we were going to do, wherever we were going to live, we would be together, at least for a while. We would be together.

CHAPTER TWO

Where in the World

If we are to live responsibly on earth, we will have to recognize that our true address is not the one listed in the phone book, but the one defined by the movement of water, the lay of the land, the dirt and air, the animals and plants, as well as by the patterns of human occupation, the buildings and crops, the language and lore. To discover our true address, we will have to . . . walk around with eyes and ears open to the neighborhood.

SCOTT RUSSELL SANDERS,
WRITING FROM THE CENTER

May 6, 1987. We're staying in Grace at Meadow Knoll, where today we took down the fence for the new road, picked up rocks, cut cedar, and cleared brush, Bill with the chain saw, I with my trusty weed-whacker, a special gift (along with a blue Swedish saw) from my husband, who obviously expects me to use these tools. I hacked away at the tangle of mustang grape and greenbrier along the edge of the woods. The vines mat into an impenetrable tangle that smothers trees and shrubs. Hard, hot work, but wonderfully satisfying to see the strong shapes of the trees emerge from the snarls and skeins and snags of climbing, clinging vines, like ideas coming clear in the writing.

September 10, 1987. Sitting in the living room of our new place, on a cool night, windows open to a breeze, talking about how we will fix things up when we have time. And there is time: it doesn't all have to be done at once. For once, I'm less interested in making the inside of the place pretty, as in decorative stuff. The land is at the center of my thoughts now, and what a good and productive shift this is, from thinking always and so deeply about self. But without that kind of self-thinking and rethinking, without the painful probing and analyzing, perhaps I couldn't be here to enjoy the land, would have been always concerned with what there is beyond what I have, would always have wanted more. Still life is what I want now. Still life, here, just here, in this place.

January 15, 1988. Got up early, walked to the lake, where we saw mallards, cormorants, a red-tailed hawk on the dead tree, a Cooper's hawk with a light belly and barred tail. The lake is low, so we could walk along the old creek bed where I imagine the Tonkawas used to camp, where raccoons have been eating mussels and crawfish and deer have come to drink. Then along the old road, beside what's left of a stone wall, back into the cedar brake. Found an old three-legged milking stool: a rough wooden round with legs made of cedar limbs, bark still on. Saw a keeled green snake by the creek and a young armadillo. No writing, but a lovely, physical day.

BY THE TIME we'd returned from the two major cross-country expeditions that occupied most of the first seven months of our marriage, we had made several important decisions about what we were going to do and where we were going to do it.

Bill had decided to leave the state agency he'd been working for. We had agreed that we would collaborate on the writing jobs that were by now regularly coming in. And yes, we wanted to live in the country. But not in any of the temptingly remote places we had visited in the Pacific Northwest and the mountain states. They were too far away, too unknown, and moving there was too difficult. Realists both (Bill more than I, certainly), we judged that staying together was an iffy proposition at best. If the marriage crashed and burned, neither of us wanted to be stranded, solo, in the wilds of Idaho or Montana.

So we would stay in Texas, at least for the time being, and move to Bill's five acres in the Hill Country. And to ratify our decision, that April afternoon in 1987, we parked Amazing Grace and christened our place Meadow Knoll, toasting our decision with the chink of a couple of soft drink cans. And that night, when the star fell, I saw it as a blessing, and was glad.

MEADOW KNOLL, which has grown from five to thirty-one acres in the two-plus decades Bill and I have been married, is located at the eastern edge of Burnet County, some sixty miles northwest of Austin, at an elevation of 1,100 feet. It lies at 30.74° north latitude, 98.05° west latitude—on the Ninety-eighth Meridian, that "institutional fault line" that Walter Prescott Webb describes as the great divide between the wooded east and the arid west. The thin soil is calcareous, weathered from the hard limestones and marly clays that were deposited in thick layers by Mesozoic seas and spangled with the fossil remains of the ancient sea creatures—*Exogyra texana*, gastropods, clams, the occasional knobby sea urchin. We often find them as we walk through the fields and along the lake, unexpected evidences of the past reaching into the present.

I sometimes imagine the advance and retreat of the seas that flooded this place during that splendid infinity: the shallow waters teeming with fish, the land blanketed with giant ferns and tropical trees, the air thick with insects, the skies alive with wings. And animals, too. The huge dinosaurs of the early Cretaceous wandered the jungles and wetlands and river deltas across this part of Texas: witness their million-year-old tracks found not far to the north, at Glen Rose. Sometimes at dawn on a steamy July day, as the sun rises over the changeless horizon, I conjure up a gigantic *Pleurocoelus* with a giraffe-like neck and sloping body, taller than a tree. Her calf at her side, she lumbers through my garden in a tropical downpour, the rain sheeting off her massive back. The ground shakes under her feet as she and her calf snack noisily on palm fronds and ferns and grasses taller than my head. She weighs more than a fully loaded eighteen-wheeler and is longer than two of Amazing Grace parked end-to-end. Her clawed hind feet could be comfortably shod with garbage can lids, it would take a block and tackle to bridle her, and only Dr. Seuss could imagine riding on her two-story-high shoulders. She's quite a girl.

Yes, well. During dinosaur days, Meadow Knoll saw a great deal more rainfall than in our era, and the plant and animal life was truly tropical. It still feels tropical, at least as far as the temperature is concerned, for a big chunk of the year. The thermometer can hover above the century mark for days, weeks at a time in the long, slow sauna of a Hill Country summer. As for rain, Meadow Knoll averages about thirty-three inches a year, which often comes two or three inches at a time, in fierce, leaf-shredding cloudbursts that wash the loose soil down to the muddy, roaring creeks.

But while this annual average tells us something, it may not tell us much. Neighboring Llano County, to the southwest, has an annual long-term average of 26.9 inches. But in 1951 the rainfall was measured at 17.64 inches, while in 1952, the county recorded 41.53 inches. Last year, Burnet County got something like 18 inches; as I'm writing this, the rainfall of the past few months has broken all records. We've received nearly 40 inches, and it's not yet August.

The rainfall may be unreliable, but the humidity here is almost always high, thanks (or no thanks) to the moisture-laden winds that sweep from the southeast, from the Gulf of Mexico, through much of the late spring and summer. Or even from the eastern Pacific, especially in El Niño seasons, when a deep plume of moisture feathers northeastward from Baja California across the mountains of Mexico into central Texas.

The winters are mild, averaging thirty-seven degrees in January. We've seen the thermometer plummet to a couple of degrees below zero when a winter storm rips southward across the plains, and one year an ice storm paralyzed the area for four days, cutting electrical power and wreaking wide havoc in our woodlot. Bill is still splitting fireplace wood from the trees brought down by the weight of that ice nearly a decade ago. But during the last decade, the climate has begun to change. Winters have been warmer, springs and autumns shorter, summers hotter, longer.

Hydrologically speaking, Meadow Knoll lies on the southern border of the thousand-mile-long Brazos River watershed, which extends from far west Texas eastward to the Gulf of Mexico, its creeks and rivers flowing northwest to southeast. Our little creek, Pecan Creek (unnamed and marked as intermittent on the map), flows into Bear Creek a mile to the southeast, and then into the San Gabriel River west of Georgetown, and after that into the Brazos River and the Gulf. This strikes people around here as odd, because the Hill Country's most significant watershed—the one that gets all the attention—is the Lower Colorado River, with its string of seven man-made flood-control and recreational lakes, draped across the Edwards Plateau some fifteen miles to the south of us. As it happens, though, there's a mini-Continental Divide between the two watersheds, just on the other side of Route 29. South, it's downhill to the Lower Colorado. North, where we are, it's downhill to the Brazos.

But that's just the surface drainage. Beneath our feet, it's an entirely different story. The water we drink comes from the region of the Texas-Oklahoma border, the headwaters of the Trinity Group aquifer, which flows southward some 550 miles in a river that ranges from 10 to 170 miles wide, through Cretaceous limestones and sandstones at varying depths beneath the surface. Here at Meadow Knoll, the aquifer is around 400 feet down—at least, that's the depth of our well.

Aquifer? Think of stacks of sponges laid end to end under the ground, each of a different thickness, different composition, different permeability. Think of rainwater percolating down from the surface, soaking the sponges. Then think of soda straws poked down to reach the water. The sponges are water-bearing rock, the straws are wells: some household wells, like ours, others irrigation wells, industrial wells, community wells.

How many wells, how much pumping, will suck an aquifer dry? What happens when drawdown exceeds recharge? These are not academic questions: ask the people who depend on the Ogallala, which stretches from South Dakota to Texas. In North Texas, the Ogallala is so dangerously depleted that it can no longer be used for irrigation, and many communities' water supplies are threatened. And to the south, where the Edwards and Trinity Aquifers supply San Antonio, there is a growing concern that water demands will soon outstrip the aquifers' supply.

Not here, though, not yet. Our Trinity water is as pure and sweet as it gets, although during dry spells it's sometimes possible to pump the well dry. When that happens, we have to stop pumping and wait until it recharges.

Geographically speaking, Meadow Knoll is situated in the northern segment of the Edwards Plateau, where two subregions meet and overlap: to the south lie the Balcones Canyonlands, an area of clear springs and creeks, limestone outcrops, caves, and steep, stony slopes bare of soil; to the north, the Lampasas Cut Plain, an extension of the southern plains, with gently rolling grass-covered hills, remnants of a vast treeless prairie that once stretched north into Canada.

This fortunate location, straddling the border of two distinct ecosystems, is known as an ecotone, a word that ecologists use to describe a transitional zone between two distinct natural communities. The area where two ecosystems overlap tends to be a richer, more complex mosaic of species, ecologically speaking, than either ecosystem alone. For example, where a woodland and a wetland intersect, you're likely to find both wetland and woodland plants and animals. Where a fencerow borders a pasture, you can find a mix of shrubs, small trees, grasses, and wildflowers. Meadow Knoll is like that, with live oaks and cedar elms and pecans and birds common to the Canyonlands, and Spanish oak and hackberry and grasses and forbs that are found on the southern plains.

To round out the mix, we've brought in other native trees from the Canyonlands. There's a golden-ball lead tree, now rare across the Edwards Plateau because the cattle and deer find it so tasty; and several dozen mountain laurels (*Sophora secundiflora*—not a true laurel) that we grew from seed pilfered from a straggly mountain laurel barely subsisting in a concrete planter on Fifth Street in Austin. I've often thought how proud that Fifth Street laurel would be if she could see her daughters. We also have several Texas redbuds and six bald cypress trees that we planted as saplings, now some thirty feet tall and producing their own offspring, which we've transplanted up and down the creek. Here at Meadow Knoll, the Canyonlands and the Cut Plains come together and overlap.

Edges, borders, overlaps. Is that what Bill and I are about? I think of Rainer Maria Rilke's remark about the kind of love in which "two solitudes protect and touch and greet each other." When we protect and touch and greet, do our edges soften and blur? Does the one influence the other, the other influence the one, so that we are no longer two separate solitudes, but one, sometimes compatibly, sometimes uncomfortably joined? How do we change each other? How do we resist change? And is it true that where and when two separate beings come together, like two ecosystems, something more complex—a third being, a both/and (rather than an either/or)—creates itself? But if this is true, how does each of us resist invasion by the other? How do we learn to be *both*, but at the same time insist on being *each*?

I think there is something important here, something central to this arrangement we call "marriage." I want to think about this.

I OFFER YOU ALL THESE geographic and other details because they were what I needed to know in order to truly situate myself, to locate myself, to discover where in the world I was when we moved to Meadow Knoll. Interestingly, and perhaps ironically, I would have no street address in this new place, the official description of which was Lot 6, Unit 3, Sunset Oaks, Bertram, Burnet County, Texas. It would be another decade before the county finally got a 911 system, requiring every property to have an address that could be located by emergency crews, and even longer before GPS coordinates replaced addresses. In the meantime, we handed out maps to friends. And because we were too far off the beaten track to get mail delivery, we rented a post office box in Bertram. We were out here alone and I loved it.

Beyond a given street address, most Americans don't really know where they are. Perhaps this is because there are so many other important things to keep track of—Internet addresses and phone numbers and itineraries and the time—or perhaps because we live and work and shop and play in so many different places. We may own a house, but this arrangement is hardly permanent or even long-term: the average American moves twelve times in his or her lifetime, and a house is more often considered an investment rather than a home place. And while real estate agents chant the mantra "location, location, location," what they're extolling is the site's relative proximity to some other, more desirable feature: shops, offices, recreation, university.

Location? Even in the age of Google Earth, most of us aren't sure where we are. Do you know your latitude and longitude? (This is the question that bedeviled the settlers who moved across the Ninety-eighth Meridian and could not understand why the rains didn't follow their plows.)

Do you know how far above sea level you live, and why you should care? (The survivors of Hurricanes Katrina and Rita might be able to tell you why.)

Do you know what watershed you live in or what aquifer you depend on, and why this matters?

Do you know who lived in your place before you came there, and who before that, and before, and before? Can you see how others' experiences of the land may have shaped the way you live, here and now?

These are not academic questions, for what we need, we humans, is to find ourselves fully and completely in place, "native to this place," as Wes Jackson puts it, and to take responsibility for the choices we make with regard to the land, to the water, to the many beings with whom we share the world.

We can only do this moment by moment, in small, incremental awakenings, discovering where we are, and why and who and even how.

But most of all, *where*.

CHAPTER THREE

Moving Through, Moving On, Moving In

I read the landscape to help me through, to know what's come before me there, to find my footing in time. The land can speak us back to ourselves, a kind of autobiography. To see it as mere scenery is like looking at the closed cover of a book.

DEBORAH TALL, *FROM WHERE WE STAND:
RECOVERING A SENSE OF PLACE*

September 15, 1987. A day of brights and darks, with strong, slanting rain, white-gold sunlight. Wind from the south, the meadow all in motion: lacy yew-willow, bronze bunches of broom-sedge, pale tracings of witchgrass, waftings of deep green purple-berried cedar, drapings of wild mustang grape and greenbrier.

November 10, 1987. Went to the library in Burnet to look up some of the county's history. I think over and over of how recently this area was settled, how violent it was here only a century ago. Turns out that the land was part of the Austin-Williams grant from the newly independent Mexican government, but was so wild and rugged that it was another quarter-century before settlers became brave enough to leave the safer areas and press westward. The Tonkawas didn't resist the incoming settlers (ranchers mostly, a few farmers), but the Comanches and Lipan Apaches were understandably resentful. Must have been tough to keep the kids and livestock safe, get supplies, make a crop, make a living. 1852, county chartered, about a thousand square miles. 1860 census, 2,387 people, including 235 slaves (69 slave owners). Earliest church, Mormon Mill, 1851. 1870 census, 281 farms. Last Indian fight in the county, 1871.

WE HUMANS LIVE chiefly in the present time, or in our own personal pasts. But the landscape is a palimpsest. Places live in all times at once (as the fossils of *Exogyra texana* teach me), and, if we are attentive and observant, we can sometimes catch a glimpse of the past or the future of a place in its present.

The first small piece of Meadow Knoll was originally a fragment of the colonization grant obtained by Robert Leftwich from the Mexican government in 1825. By the turn of the century it had become part of the thousand-acre Russell Ranch. (If the Russells in the 1860 and 1870 Burnet County census are connected with this ranch—their occupation is listed as stock raisers—they originally came from Missouri.) In the early 1970s, the ranch was bought by a developer and carved up into three-acre lots.

By the time Bill arrived in 1974, a century of ruinous overgrazing and the long drought of the 1950s had nearly destroyed the native grasses, and there were only a few live oaks, pecans, and cedar along the creek, with mesquite and cedar scattered elsewhere. The land still testifies to its earlier incarnation as a ranch: the wheel tracks of the ranch wagons that crossed Meadow Knoll from one corner to another remain visible, worn deep into a shelf of limestone where it crosses the creek. We've found other relics, too: stone walls, dry-laid across the fields; an iron wagon wheel; a couple of iron cowbells, pitted with rust; a three-legged milking stool with cedar branches for legs; the blade of a wooden plane, used to smooth boards rough-cut in a local sawmill. A rusted plow blade and the earthen terraces that crisscross the northern section are evidence of cotton farming, probably before the First World War. And after a flood had scoured the mud out of a deep pool in the creek, Bill discovered the pieces of a large broken crock. Was it used to cool butter and eggs in the flowing water? Or was it part of a whiskey still, smashed when the revenuers raided the "joint," as such things were called hereabouts? The Feds would have taken the copper, which was good as gold during the Depression, and still is.

The cows were rounded up and moved out in the 1970s, and seasons of rain have brought back the native grasses: bluestem, turkeyfoot bluestem, sideoats grama, curly mesquite, love grass. The meadows host Ashe junipers (known locally as cedar), mesquite, and—in marshy places—willow and cypress. The woodlot (called a "motte," defined as a place where trees grow closely together) is full of oak, elm, hackberry, mulberry, and pecan—firewood that heats the house through the winter. The climate is changing again (I write on the cusp of man-made global warming) and another millennium may bring a desert or a jungle, or even an encroaching sea. But for now, this is a lovely, welcoming place.

And unpeopled, or relatively so, for the land in the vicinity of Meadow Knoll, as in all of Burnet County, has seen permanent human settlement only since the 1850s. But there have been tourists here for some twelve thousand years, wanderers moving through, moving on. The Paleo-American people of Texas, like the elephants, mastodons, camels, and bison they hunted, were a roving sort. They set up temporary camps beside the springs and along the rivers, where their Clovis-like stone tools and human remains have been found. After them came other nomads, the buffalo-hunting, teepee-building Tonkawa Indians who traveled across these hills until the end of the nineteenth century and are now all but forgotten.

At the end of Indian Wells Road, along the western border of the property we added to Meadow Knoll in 1999, lies a seventeen-acre man-made lake. We call it Indian Wells Lake, although it doesn't appear by that name on any map. It drowned what was likely a Tonkawa campground beside a cluster of artesian springs—Indian wells. The lake was created by an ignorant, uncaring developer with a large bulldozer, perhaps imagining that a fishing lake would increase the property values of his subdivision. He bladed up enough rocks and soil to dam the creek, destroying whatever artifacts and life-traces the Indians might have left behind. The lake, predictably silting up at the west (intake) end, empties and fills with the seasonal rains, sometimes shrinking to a puddle the size of a swimming pool, other times brimful and spilling over, enjoyed by catfish, wading birds, and migratory ducks.

On this day, Indian Wells Lake is full, and as I walk along the shore, watching the kingfishers diving, the heron still as a poised sword in the shallows, I imagine the Tonkawas on a warm day in October, under a blue sky filled with coasting clouds like white bubbles of foam. The rise I stand on overlooks a campground full of Tonkawa women clad in short deerskin skirts, trailed by laughing, dancing Tonkawa children, their heads flattened in the style of that tribe, clad in nothing at all. A few men are clustered in small groups, telling stories as they chip arrowheads and spear points from the flint nodules they've found in the Edwards Plateau limestone or picked up from gravel deposits along their route of travel. There are dogs underfoot everywhere, and ponies tethered for grazing, and on the other side of the clear artesian springs bubbling up out of the rocks, I see a conical brush hut that has been erected as a temporary refuge for menstruating women.

This is the Acorn Clan, related through their mothers, since the Tonkawa are not only a matrilineal but also a matrilocal people. Their squat buffalo hide teepees encircle the open area and smoke from their fires curls lazily into the clear air. Some of the women are fleshing a deerskin the men have brought into the camp. Others are stirring pots of squirrel stew over campfires, or chopping the pads of prickly pear cacti, or smoking the fish they have netted in pools farther down the creek, or weaving rushes into mats and sandals. The older children chant songs with no melody as they use rocks to crack the pecans they have gathered from the ancestors of the pecan trees now growing in our woodlot. The Acorn Clan has no garden or agricultural enterprise, but the land through which they travel—their home—offers everything they need, abundantly. The group is peaceful and happy, although some of the women are disturbed by a report that a Comanche raiding party has been seen to the north, near the Brazos River.

As well they might be. The Spanish borrowed the word *Komantcia* from the Utes, for whom it meant "someone who wants to fight me all the time." This is an accurate description of the fierce Plains nomads, mounted on their horses and armed with spears, bows, and—after about 1750—guns. They harried the less aggressive Tonkawa, stole their horses, and took their children and women captive, aiming (with eventual success and some help from white settlers) to drive them from their home range.

Did that invading band of braves raid the Tonkawa camp at Indian Wells, just on the other side of those willows, just there? If I listen hard enough on a night when the Comanche moon is full and bright, will I hear the howls of the attackers and the anguished cries of women and children as the Comanches take what they want and ride off into the night? And while I'm thinking of violent scenes like these, wasn't it Comanches who ambushed and murdered the Wofford Johnson family—father, mother, and an eight-year-old girl—on their way home from a neighbor's place, where they had been making molasses from their homegrown crop of sorghum? The massacre took place only a few miles to the south of us, near the village of Hopewell. Meadow Knoll is tranquil now and our neighborhood crime rate, happily, is very low. But it was not always so.

Yes, there were massacres and murder, although it isn't fair to heap all the blame on the Comanches, who were responding to the federal government's slaughter of the buffalo and the loss of the territory they themselves had taken from the defenseless Tonkawas.

And it certainly isn't fair of me to call the Tonkawas "tourists," for while they did not settle in one place, they were scarcely visitors. For centuries, they and their ancestors moved through all of what is now Central Texas as knowingly as the foxes and mountain lions and owls. They knew its hills and canyons and river bottoms intimately, knew every native berry, every edible root, every healing herb. They knew the nature of the land, its geography, its history of human habitation. They knew where their ancestors were buried and held those places sacred. For them, the landscape itself would have been a teller of tales. That hill, this creek, those trees—each had a story, carried in the mind as a loving and instructive presence. Until the Comanches drove them from it, this was their home ground, richly storied, profoundly meaningful.

The Comanches were a serious threat. To provide some degree of protection to anybody who was fool enough to risk settling here, the Texas Rangers built Fort Croghan about fifteen miles west, manned by federal troops in 1849. Within a few years, enough foolhardy settlers had moved west from the safer environs of Austin to create a new county, Burnet County, which got its first post office in 1858. The buffalo hunters had finished their bloody business by 1870, and the Comanches and other Indians whose lives depended on the bison were corralled by soldiers and herded onto reservations. The railroad line between Austin and Burnet was laid in 1882, and the village of Bertram, where Bill and I go to pick up our mail, was established as a shipping depot for wool and cowhides. The settlement was originally founded some two miles to the southwest, but when the new railroad passed it by, the disappointed villagers hitched up their oxen and towed their log cabins three miles north, where they rebuilt their town. It's said that one lady settler, unhurried, unmoved, sat in her rocking chair in the doorway, knitting, as her cabin hustled northward.

By the 1890s, the new village boasted a post office, a cotton gin and gristmill, three general stores, a grocer, a blacksmith, a shoemaker, and two wagon makers. The soil wasn't exceptionally fertile to start with and there wasn't enough rain to support the kind of crops that settlers were used to, coming from east of the Ninety-eighth Meridian. But farmers on this "prodigal frontier," as John Graves calls it, managed to grow enough cotton on the flats along the creeks to deplete whatever humus there might have been. And the ranchers put so many cows, sheep, and goats on the land that the rich grass was gnawed to the root. The grass cover destroyed, its holding power gone forever, the unforgiving sun and wind dried the soil to a fine powder and the fierce rains washed it off the hills and into the streams.

But for a while, the little town flourished. Traffic in local cotton, cattle, sheep, and goats made Bertram the major railway shipping point for the eastern part of Burnet County. The population boomed, reaching one thousand in 1929, and there was enough commercial activity to support four banks, four filling stations, four cotton gins (no doubt about it, cotton was king), three barbershops, and two lumberyards. But the prosperity was temporary. The Crash took down all but one of the banks, and the bottom dropped out of the cotton market just about the time the boll weevil moved into the neighborhood, followed by the Depression. World War II took all the able-bodied young men and didn't send many back, and the drought of the 1950s just about finished off the town. A few tenacious folks, deeply rooted, held on, but most of the people, like the soil, dried up and blew away. The land emptied, and the town barely clung to life.

But that's changing. Relatively speaking, Burnet County is still sparsely populated, with some forty-two thousand people spread out over a thousand square miles, most living in Marble Falls, Burnet (the county seat), and Bertram, others scattered up and down a network of unimproved caliche roads spiderwebbing across the Hill Country. But Travis and Williamson Counties, neighbors to the east, have a combined population of nearly 1.5 million people in about 4,000 square miles, and both are among the dozen or so fastest-growing counties in the nation. The local real estate folks are hoping that these crowds will spill over into Burnet County's empty spaces.

They won't have long to wait. The urban blight that has infected the I-35 corridor is spreading faster than boll weevils, its asphalt tide lapping westward along Routes 183 and 29. The McDonalds and Bed Bath & Beyonds have not yet reached our edge of the county, but once-open range and cotton fields are sprouting upscale subdivisions and exclusive gated communities. Wal-Mart can't be far behind.

There's an irony in this, of course. For part of what is driving this movement is the perception that rural regions like the Hill Country are rich in the tradition and sense of rootedness that most modern, mobile Americans lack. What people are looking for is not just a house, not just their own half-acre, but also a connection to past and place. In *Places in the World a Person Could Walk*, David Syring writes:

> A friend from Houston once told me that the Hill Country is where most
> Texans would choose to live if they could pick anywhere in the state. If
> you come from East Texas, my friend told me, you love the feeling of
> space and openness the region gives. When you rise up out of the humid
> coastal plain above the Balcones Escarpment, my friend said, you can just

feel yourself getting healthier. When you approach the area from the west, the small, well-kept towns remind you civilization does exist in Texas, and the startling sight of spring-fed streams and rivers soaks into you like a cold drink for your parched West Texas soul.[4]

Sometimes, watching the bulldozers and the building and the landscaped boulevards, I feel as if all of Texas, north, south, east, west, is converging on us.

But not yet, not quite. For all the nomadic traipsing across this area over the centuries, the comings and goings of prehistoric and historic peoples, and the threat of a modern invasion by the clamoring crowds of suburbia, the area right around Meadow Knoll has remained relatively empty, until recently, that is. When Bill bought this place, the nearest neighbor was a couple of miles away. By the time we moved here, Dee and Rick and their children Greg and Terry were living in a single-wide on the fifteen acres to the north. Robbie, a hobby rancher, ran cows and goats and a horse on the eighteen acres adjacent to the lake and weekended there with his wife Jackie and their children and grand-children. But the Ramsey and Baum Ranches to the south and east were open range, eight thousand acres that were home to deer, coyotes, mountain lions, and a herd of longhorn cows that used to hang their heads over the fence and stare at Grace, parked on her green knoll.

Land has been relatively cheap here (a situation that has recently changed), and over the years, more people have moved in. There are houses along both sides of Indian Wells and Lakeshore roads, but the area east of the lake, where we live, has actually been depopulated. Rick and Dee got a double-wide, then gave it back to the bank and brought in a single-wide. Greg got married and in-stalled a double-wide on the three acres farthest to the north, against the Ram-sey Ranch fence. Terry and her girlfriend put a single-wide on the three acres next door and had a baby. Lamont and Marge, Rick's parents, put a single-wide, then a triple-wide on the three acres nearest to us. Then Greg got a divorce and Terry and her girlfriend split. Dee and Rick and the girlfriend's baby and Lam-ont and Marge all moved elsewhere, taking all four of their trailers with them and selling us most of their property. (Their departure was especially welcome because Rick, Greg, and Lamont were truckers and their eighteen-wheelers chewed up the unimproved gravel road.) Sadly, Robbie died of cancer; Jackie was glad to find buyers—Bill and I—who cared for the land as much as her husband had. By the end of the '90s, our five acres had become thirty-one. And even though the Baum and Ramsey ranches have been sold off in twenty-five-acre parcels, we can't see any of the three or four houses out there.

Sadly, the nomads who live west of the lake don't always care about the land, and there are no ordinances to keep them from using and abusing it as they please. There's an ugly junkyard on Indian Wells Road, and the woman who bought the three acres west of the lake stripped off all the topsoil, dug a hole the size of a house in one corner, and filled it with discarded refrigerators and mattresses and other such junk. As it turns out, she is a true nomad: last week, I drove past and saw that her house, a double-wide, is gone.

Since this is largely a nomadic community, it's not much of a community. Most of the people will tell you that they've left the restrictions of the city and moved to the freedom of the country so they can live exactly as they please. This may mean permitting their helmet-less third graders to ride dirt bikes and ATVs on the road and on property belonging to absentee owners, or freeing their Dobermans to terrorize the neighbors' sheep and geese, or trying to keep goats with a bad fence, or burning trash on windy days when the humidity is in the teens and the grass is like straw. It may also mean setting up a deer blind so that the target area includes a neighbor's property, or firing a twelve-gauge at mourning doves perched on a neighbor's telephone wire. It may even mean building a private fence a dozen feet into the public right-of-way.

But we live at the far end of a dead-end road, on the far side of the lake, and these irritations are mostly minor and transitory, in part because people move in, stay a while, and move on. The kid who shot up the telephone line grew up and joined the army, the ATV broke down and hasn't been fixed, and the man with the goats and the bad fence is dead.

Texans are known for their brash and independent spirit, and the nomads around here don't take kindly to suggestions. To a city dweller, this intransigence may seem to translate to "somebody who wants to fight me all the time." But so far this rural neighborhood has been relatively safe, with meth labs the most imminent danger. (Fifteen labs were seized in the county in 2003, the last year for which statistics are available.) It may be the armed citizenry, with its twelve-gauge shotguns and its undisciplined Dobermans, that's keeping it this way. You'd have to be crazy to pull into a driveway or down a country lane after dark around here.

Somebody might just shoot you.

CHAPTER FOUR

Dwelling, Rooting, Learning

As much as we live in a place, we live in *place*; we inhabit a condition of the soul. . . . We live where we have made definitions, and in the process of making definitions, we create a place in which to live.

SALLIE TISDALE, *STEPPING WESTWARD: THE LONG SEARCH FOR HOME IN THE PACIFIC NORTHWEST*

Home is where we have a history.

TERRY TEMPEST WILLIAMS,
A VOICE IN THE WILDERNESS

February 3, 1988. Reading Milton Myeroff, On Caring: "We are 'in place' in the world through having our lives ordered by inclusive caring. This is in contrast with being 'out of place,' trying to escape from the 'wrong place,' and indifference and insensibility to place."

March 12, 1988. Cleared brush along the creek, helped Bill hang a gate and string fence wire at the turnaround. The hog plum in full, sweet bloom in the woods, to the delight of the bees, and the smaller Chickasaw plum, in Lazarus' Meadow, where we've hung a bluebird box. Heard, then saw, two huge flocks of sandhill cranes heading north, calling in that wild chortling gabble that always makes me cry for sheer joy.

April 20, 1988. Hard to push myself indoors to work in such a lovely spring, but need to get the book finished. Revised two more chapters today, should be done by next week, and ready to go on to the next project (another Nancy Drew). Sitting on the porch now, in the dusk, listening to the quiet. Well, not very. There's the incessant whistle of a titmouse, high-pitched and monotonous, Johnny one-note. A cow far away, the great horned owl with his low who-whoo, closer. A plane, the train on the other side of the hill, a crow, several crows, a mourning dove. And that titmouse.

September 19, 1988. Reading Peter Matthiessen's The Snow Leopard: *"And perhaps this is what Tukten knows—that the journey to the Dolpo, step by step and day by day, is the Jewel in the Heart of the Lotus, the Tao, the Way, the Path, but no more so than the small events of days at home." Small events, ordinary doings, dailiness. The way, the path.*

FOR SEVERAL MONTHS in the spring of 1987, Bill and I commuted from the house in northwest Austin to Amazing Grace, who, although sadly deficient in closets, was a convenient dwelling for two people who liked being close. Bill and I were already working together on young adult writing assignments (we did five books that first year, in spite of the traveling). But we spent as much time as we could at Meadow Knoll, living in Grace, busy with the tasks of setting up a permanent home at Meadow Knoll. Grace was fine for the short haul, but she was a little cramped for long-term living, especially considering the space required by two large cats: Orange Julius (OJ), the sweetest orange tabby you'd ever hope to meet, and PK, an imperious Siamese who was later reincarnated as Khat, the shop cat in the China Bayles mystery series.

What had to be done at Meadow Knoll required months of hard, physical labor. We laid down a two-track gravel lane across the rocky pasture from the point where the road ended. We took out a couple of interior fences. (Handling rusty barbed wire that's been stapled in place for a half century is like wrestling with rattlesnakes.) Bill arranged for utility poles to be installed from the point where the electrical and phone lines dead-ended at Dee and Rick's place and connected the house to the new meter. Amazing Grace towed Bill's bachelor cabin out of the woods and onto the top of the knoll, to be wired for electricity and used for storage. (I was reminded of those hardy Bertram oxen, towing the pioneers' houses to their new town site.)

Most daunting of all was installing the septic tank. I'd lived with privies when I was a kid on the farm, but as an adult, all I'd had to do was flush. It never occurred to me to wonder what happened to all that stuff after it disappeared down the drain. I was about to learn.

For the mechanical labor, Bill rented a backhoe, a yellow machine the size of a baby *Pleurocoelus*, fitted with a scoop-blade up front and a crab-claw digger behind. He dug a five-by-eight-foot pit, six feet deep, for the thousand-gallon tank (in which the solids in "all that stuff" are gobbled up by greedy anaerobic bacteria) and a fifty-yard looping trench for the leach pipes—perforated pipe that allows the liquid stuff to drain out of the tank and into the soil. Some guys in a big truck brought the concrete tank and neatly dropped it in, a square plug in a square just-the-right-size hole. Bill buried it. I filled the leach trench with septic rock, a back-breaking job that gave me plenty of time to contemplate the hard facts of life in the country. In this labor, Bill and I were assisted by whatever volunteer helpers happened to drop in on a given day—a very few, actually, since friends and family wisely preferred not to spend their Sundays on the business end of a shovel. Most of the work we did, we did together, alone.

If you've ever buried anything bigger than a breadbox, you'll have some idea of just how hard all this was. I hate to wear gloves, and when my husband caught me looking ruefully at my ruined nails, he'd ask (one eyebrow raised and with his most sardonic Bill Albert grin) if I was getting what I wanted. He was testing me, I thought. I'd always answer yes, even when I didn't know whether it was true.

By late August, the leach trench was filled, the utilities were ready, and we went shopping for a house. A few days later, we'd found what we wanted—more accurately, what we could afford. It was scheduled for delivery in another week.

Neither of us had ever lived in a mobile home (the itinerant Amazing Grace excepted), but as we looked over our finances, considered the time and effort involved in building, and pondered the uncertainties of this untested marriage, a trailer was our best option. While we each had fallback savings and the writing work seemed reliable enough, saddling ourselves with a mortgage did not seem like a Good Plan.

So we looked for and found a used single-wide. Called Sammy (for no good reason), the trailer was 12 feet wide and 58 feet long, for a total of 696 square feet of living space—just a little larger than the graduate student housing where the kids and I lived while I was studying at Berkeley. Our Austin house was the standard three-bedroom-two-bath-attached-garage. It was full. A single-wide was definitely going to be a tight fit.

But as a dwelling, Sammy had his virtues. A wide kitchen window with a view of the south meadow. Another wide window in my writing studio, looking out into a dense cedar brake busy with cardinals, titmice, and jays. A living room window facing east to the sunrise and a patio door that opened onto the porch that Bill built, overlooking the grassy slope westward, down to the creek.

What's more, Sammy was definitely affordable, which is to say cheap. Bill wrote a check for forty-five hundred dollars plus tax and gave the salesman a map and directions to Grace's knoll. Grace (who was ready to retire after a long, hard life on the road) found another place to park, and Sammy arrived and was installed without incident on the knoll, under the astonished gaze of the longhorns watching through the fence. We celebrated our first wedding anniversary in our new home, with a bottle of bubbly.

This wasn't Thoreau's cabin, and I was glad of it. We had a phone and electricity. We also had a heater, an air conditioner (essential if you want to spend summers in the Texas Hill Country), a refrigerator, a large freezer, and a television set with an antenna that picked up four Austin channels, sometimes. No cable, no mail delivery, no Internet (not invented yet), no fast food closer than fifty round-trip miles and no supermarket closer than thirty. We had a dining/work table, a sofa, a double bed, desks and desktop computers (laptops hadn't been invented yet, either), and an assortment of chairs.

But we didn't have a well. Drilling four hundred feet down to the Trinity aquifer and installing pipe and a pump would cost as much as we had just spent to put a roof over our heads, so for the rest of that year and most of the next, we hauled water from town for drinking and cooking and water from the creek for flushing.

We hadn't entirely moved in yet, either. Because the only thing we could count on was that our publishers' checks would be late (a fact of that early writing life), both of us had part-time jobs that fall. I taught a couple of freshman composition courses at Austin Community College and Southwest Texas State, and Bill was substituting in the Austin schools. We planned to keep the house in Austin through the spring, a comfort station where we could take showers and do the laundry, and where the cats could stay until we were settled in.

For me, none of these minor inconveniences mattered very much. I spent as much time as I could at Meadow Knoll, where the rising sun spoke its invocation to each new day, the noon sky shimmered with a glorious, soul-searing heat, and the night worked a vast and wondrous alchemy, turning the sky to liquid black and scattering it with stars. I was alone there. Or when Bill was with me, we were alone together.

"NOTHING CAN GROW unless it taps into the soil," William Carlos Williams says in his *Autobiography*. Humans need places in which, like plants, they can root themselves, be in touch with the soil, with the landscape around them.

But more and more people live in cities. They work in buildings that are insulated from the earth by floors, walled from the wind, and roofed from the rain. When it's time to go home, they walk on pavements to the parking lot, drive their cars to their residential suburbs, park in garages, and step into houses, often without going outdoors. If they have any awareness of place, it's an outsider's awareness of the houses they pass on the street, the buildings in the vicinity of work, school, and shopping, the highways along which they commute—human-made artifacts that dominate our human-shaped environments. When they go on vacation, they're tourists, seeing the country through car windows as they speed along, skimming the deserts and mountains with a glance. They are surrounded by landscapes, by scenery, but they have no authentic sense of place.

What's more, these places, and the people in them, are mutable. Neighbors and coworkers come, stay for a while, then go. Stores change hands, restaurants open and close, old shopping malls are bulldozed and new ones pop up in time for the holiday blitzkrieg. Generally speaking, we are as nomadic as the Tonkawas. Everything is temporary, in transition, short-term, contingent. Nothing is permanent. Nothing lasts.

My life had been like that. When I was a child, my family moved from one rented house to another, a year here, eighteen months there, never more than two years in one place. (Perhaps it was no accident that I read to tatters the *Little House* books. The Ingalls' itinerate pioneer life, their restless migrations from one prairie settlement to another, was something I could understand.) As an adult, I was constantly on the move. I lived in campus housing, tiny apartments, larger apartments, condos without yards, houses with yards, and several splendidly upscale houses in exclusive neighborhoods. I no sooner began to feel at home than it was time to up sticks and move.

My relationships were almost as peripatetic and temporary. My first marriage to Bob, the father of our three children, broke up when we moved from our home territory in Illinois to the unsettling, radically unstable world that was Berkeley in the late 60s. A second marriage—one of those impulsive, what-was-she-thinking affairs—ended after a turbulent two months. The third, to Jim, a talented architect, lasted as long as the first, but ended in divorce about the time I moved to Southwest Texas State.

You don't divorce your kids, so my children, now grown, have formed the stable base of my relational life for nearly five decades. But otherwise, there was nothing in my adult experience of places, houses, or spouses to suggest that permanency would ever be important to me. I've never asked Bill if he wondered whether I was a good bet as a marriage partner, but I wouldn't have blamed him for being skeptical when I said that fidelity—to a person, to a home place, to an undistinguished five-acre patch of ground—was something I hungered for. He might have thought that this, too, was a fleeting desire and that I was just another nomad, on my way somewhere else.

But I was telling the truth. The deepest, truest part of me wanted to be rooted, to be connected, to stay put, to *dwell*. There is some irony, of course, in the fact that the place in which I had chosen to root myself had previously hosted only migrants and nomads. And that the house in which I chose to live still had its axles and wheels stored underneath.

Wheels or no wheels, Sammy was a very fine dwelling for the nearly eight years we lived in him. He was a refuge from storms, sheltered a sometimes stormy marriage, and offered faithful sanctuary. On his knoll, under the oaks, his hitch overgrown with honeysuckle, roses climbing over the windows, he became an integral part of the landscape—and still is, now in use as a craft studio, a library, and a storage place for the things other people stow in their basements and attics.

Sammy is well-endowed with windows and doors, and living there was almost like living in a glassed-in pavilion, open on all sides to the land. Sometimes this accessibility to the native wildlife proved startling. We skirted the trailer with plywood, but possums and raccoons and even a skunk took up temporary residence underneath. One night in our third or fourth year there, I found a baby possum, no bigger than a teacup, cuddled up to my sleeping husband's foot, under the covers of our bed. Squirrels, despite Bill's most creative opposition, persisted in building their nests in the space between the roof and the ceiling and inviting their friends for midnight capers while we were trying to sleep. Hummingbirds flew in and couldn't fly out unless we caught and escorted them to the door. The cats invited bunnies and rats indoors, then got busy with something else and forgot about them. Field mice took liberties with the contents of the cupboards. Scorpions liked to hang around the bathroom, and it was smart to look before you stepped in for a shower.

Sammy couldn't protect us from every storm. There was sometimes anger and pain, grief and loss and fear and a failure of vision. But this is true of all houses, every home, whether teepee or trailer or Taj Mahal. And eventually, no matter how far apart we fell in those times of anger and pain, we always came together again. Together, alone and together, again.

OVER THE YEARS, I've walked every inch of Meadow Knoll, the open fields and the densest cedar brakes, rooting myself in this place, grounding myself in its seasonal changes: the too-short springs; the too-long, too-hot summers; the glorious autumns and mild gray winters. Every day, often before the sun comes up, the dogs and I—three dogs, for many of those years, a heeler named Toro and black Labs Zach and Lady—do an early morning walkabout.

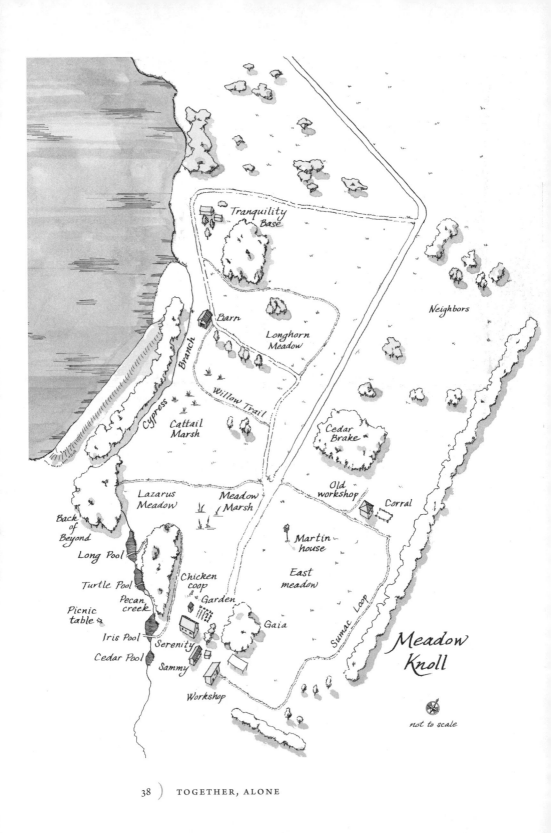

Tranquility
Base

Neighbors

Barn

Longhorn
Meadow

Cypress
Branch

Willow Trail

Cattail
Marsh

Cedar
Brake

Old
workshop

Corral

Lazarus
Meadow

Meadow
Marsh

Back
of
Beyond

Martin
house

Long Pool

Chicken
coop

East
meadow

Turtle Pool

Garden

Pecan
creek

Picnic
table

Gaia

Iris Pool

Serenity

Cedar Pool

Sammy

Workshop

Sumac Loop

Meadow
Knoll

not to scale

One of my favorite paths takes me across the footbridge over Iris Pool, under one of the half-dozen cypress trees we planted twenty years ago. Yellow flags bloom here in April, and Louisiana iris, all colors. The path takes me along Pecan Creek, heading generally north, with a fringe of woodland on the right and open meadow on the left, where we have a picnic table. In spring, the meadow is a basin of bluebonnets; in autumn, a gaiety of purple gayfeather and prickly eryngo, a thistle look-alike that keeps its brilliant lavender color in dried bouquets. We may see wild turkeys or deer. We'll hear a cardinal calling, clear and shrill, or the rusty clatter of a yellow-billed cuckoo or the plaintive two-note of a bob-white, too few, sadly, since fire ants kill the young of ground-nesting birds like bob-whites and roadrunners.

The dogs racing ahead, I cross the creek again at the footbridge over Long Pool, on the outskirts of the untamed, unruly Back of Beyond, duck through the fence between the yaupon holly and the mulberry tree, and head along Cypress Branch, the intermittent drainage from the lake. There are wild pecan trees on the left, and a tangled snarl of elbow bush, Southern blackhaw, button bush (the great delight of bees), and rough-leafed dogwood, white-berried in July and August. This is a marshy area, where we've planted eight or nine second-generation cypress trees grown from seed, offspring of those we planted twenty years ago. In another twenty years, these cypress will shade the ground beneath, and this will become a darker, more mysterious place. The dogs are always busy here, noses to the ground, for deer bed down in the sedge, and their scent hangs heavy everywhere.

But the way ahead is soggy from recent rains, so we turn east, toward the sunrise. Like white smoke, the morning fog wisps and curls where the ground is damp and the temperature lower. The dogs lope off in pursuit of a fugitive rabbit but catch up to me as I cross a small stream that flows into the nearby cattail marsh.

The cattail is a ruthless invader, but generous, for all that. Indians dug the rhizomes for food and wove the leaves into mats and baskets and sandals and used them to built huts and thatch roofs. They stripped the stem fibers and twisted them into cords and stuffed the white seed fluff into moccasins for warmth. One Indian tribe's name for cattail was translated as "plant for papoose's bed": the fluffy masses of seeds are soft and do not mat. During World War II, several million pounds of seed pods were collected and used to stuff life jackets, flight suits, mattresses, and pillows.

The cattail marsh is ringed by a fringe of five-foot-high yew willows, so called for its narrow leaves. *Baccharis neglecta* is its Latin name. It also goes by poverty weed, Roosevelt weed, New Deal weed. New Deal weed? I was curious enough about this to look it up. I learned that the name likely comes from the make-work days of the New Deal, when the yew willow (which grows readily in waste places, hence the species name *neglecta)* was widely planted to control erosion. The genus name *Baccharis* comes from Bacchus, the Greek god of wine, because the roots of plants in this large group (some three hundred and fifty species worldwide) were once used to "flavor wine."

"Flavor wine" was something of a puzzler until I read (in Daniel Moerman's *Native American Ethnobotany)* that the Hualapai Indians made a cold infusion of the plant's roots to bathe the temples as a headache treatment. So maybe I shouldn't be surprised that the plant is named for Bacchus: I can imagine the roots bruised and steeped in wine to treat headaches and maybe even hangovers, caused (of course) by a bacchanalian revel. According to Moerman, *Baccharis sp.* has seen other interesting uses: it has been taken for stomachaches, applied as a wound medicine or to reduce swelling, used as a treatment for gonorrhea and kidney ailments, made into a liniment for rheumatism, employed as a "ceremonial emetic," an eyewash, and a remedy for baldness. Oh, and the Mojave and Yuma roasted and ate the young shoots as a "starvation food." Ah, yes—there it is, starvation food, poverty weed. Every American Indian tribe seems to have turned its local *Baccharis* into something useful.

Around here, though, ranchers don't like this large, fast-growing shrub, which thrives on neglect and colonizes soils that most other plants its size don't enjoy. It's not a shrub you'd want in a landscape, either, because the weak stems and branches break easily and it's only pretty for the few weeks it's in bloom. But if you ask a bee or wasp or beetle or butterfly what they think about this weed, you'll get an earful. In September and October, the yew willows are covered with fuzzy white blossoms that summon every bug with a sweet tooth for miles around. It's a delight to stand in a poverty weed patch and listen to the buzzing of happy insects sipping the nourishing *neglecta* nectar.

I'm from the Midwest and have lovely memories of farm ponds, deep and cool and dark, home to catfish and perch. So I once proposed that we build a pond in this marshy spot—a tank, as Texans call such things—where we could swim and fish. But Bill pointed out that the substrate was too porous to contain the surface water that makes its way here and that most of the year we'd have a large, empty hole, definitely not a place for fish. So the cattails and yew willows live on, happily wet-footed, inviting the nectaring insects in September and October and the red-winged blackbirds that spill their music in April and May. A fair trade, I think. As good as a pond, or nearly. As close to a pond as I'm likely to get, anyway.

A bit farther along, by the gate, Texas and Blossom, our longhorn cow and her calf, amble over to greet us, a little nervously because the heeler knows it's his job to keep everybody on the move. There's a brief and noisy exchange through the fence before the dogs lose interest and the cows go back to their grazing.

We've reached the gravel lane. Sometimes we turn and walk back home, past the purple martin house and our wooden Meadow Knoll sign and the stand of Lindheimer's muhly, a lovely native perennial bunch grass. Cattle find it so delicious that it's disappeared from the pastures and survives only where they can't get at it—in my garden and along the creek. But sometimes we head straight east, up what used to be our neighbor's driveway. To the left, there's a big patch of sunflowers and Mexican hat where Dee and Rick's trailer was parked, and a mown circle where Bill burns brush. (There's a spigot here, part of the old water system, which is a good safeguard when he's burning.) Ahead on the left is an abandoned workshop, cobbled together out of scrap lumber and roofed with tarpaper, not built to last, not good for much now. Behind it is the fenced corral where horses and pigs lived, and around it, in the summer, there's a thick stand of squaw-weed. Growing with the squaw-weed is a huge buffalo gourd (*Cucurbita foetidissima*), whose genus name groups it with squashes and cucumbers and the like and whose species name exactly describes the smell of the crushed leaves: fetid.

Both squaw-weed and buffalo gourd were used by Native Americans as abortifacients—plants whose chemicals can cause uterine contractions intense enough to abort an early-stage fetus. The buffalo gourd was also employed by Indian mothers to wean their babies: the juice smeared on a nipple would be a definite deterrent to nursing. This squash-like plant produces a large crop of bitter, inedible fruits that the Indians dried and used as containers and scoops. The young fruits and the seeds, however, are edible, and the local rodents find them irresistible. By mid-winter, there's not a whole gourd in sight, but turn over a rock and you're likely to discover a cache of dried seeds, carefully hoarded against leaner times.

Here, summer's squaw-weed is replaced by a spectacular autumn goldenrod. The genus name of this remarkable plant, *Solidago*, means "to make whole"; it been used as a healing herb since ancient times. The goldenrod market perked up when *Solidago* was discovered growing in great plenty in the American colonies. The colonists cut and dried the plant, baled it, and shipped it to England, where it was sold in the apothecary shops. Traveling all those miles, it was pricey: two ounces of goldenrod might fetch a gold crown.

For Native Americans, goldenrod was free. It was a staple medicine, and since some two dozen species grow across the continent, nearly every tribe was within arm's reach of at least one. Called "sun medicine," it was used to treat everything from wounds and fevers to rheumatism and toothache. It was also used as a charm, smoked like tobacco, woven into baskets, burned as incense, and made into a dye. And if that's not enough to demonstrate the significance of this golden plant, consider this: learning that goldenrod sap contained a natural latex, Thomas Edison, that relentless inventor, bred the plant to increase its latex yield. He then produced a resilient, long-lasting rubber that Henry Ford made into a set of tires for his own personal automobile. Edison was still experimenting with this rubber when he died in 1931. His research was turned over to the U.S. government, which apparently found it of little importance, even when rubber became almost impossible to get during World War II. Goldenrod rubber. Fancy that.

But the dogs and I are moving on. Bill is an amateur blacksmith and over there, behind the old workshop, is a pile of rusty scrap iron for his forge. Things that look to me like they belong in the dump look to him like gold. Who am I to judge? Next to his stash of scrap iron is my stash of scrap brick, which I've mined for a brick patio and walks and garden edgings at the house.

And just past the twin hoards of scrap iron and bricks is our stack of split firewood, enough for several seasons. Through the year, Bill cuts dead trees and saws them into usable lengths. In November, when it's cool, we rent a log-splitter and spend a day or two together, splitting and hauling firewood, mostly oak, some hackberry, some cedar, stacking it to dry for a year or two or three. The winters here are mild enough and our house (the house that replaced Sammy a few years ago) is small and compact enough so that a fire in the fireplace heats the whole place. And as I put another log on the fire on a winter's night, I like to think of that warming work, and of the fifty or sixty years of sunlight that lit the leaves and fired the sap and fueled the roots of the tree, all released now, in flames that warm my bones and fire my spirit. "And with each gust a wisp of smoke from my chimney bears witness," Aldo Leopold says, "to whomsoever it may concern, that the sun did not shine in vain." Such a generous abundance this world offers, such a wealth of gifts.

Farther east, the path makes a sharp corner back to the south. There's a hole in the fence here, the wires deliberately snipped so that creatures—foxes, raccoons, possums, coyotes, and the like—can come through on their nocturnal travels. I have to keep an eye on the dogs. If I let them, they'll slip through the fence and be off like a shot, down to the creek, to the woods, to a neighbor's tank, and it'll be an hour or more before I see them again. So I speak sternly and keep the heeler on his leash until we've passed temptation by.

There's always a lot of traffic through this fence. I see coon prints on the path this morning, and the narrow, five-clawed prints of an armadillo. And just here, last summer, a coyote deposited a couple of long gray cartridges of scat, studded with tiny white bones and bits of felted fur. Inside one, I found a single small, perfect claw.

Unlike the other pastures at Meadow Knoll, the East Meadow—the field we're walking through—bears no evidence of having been plowed. Dee pastured a pair of burros here. They grazed it heavily, but that was ten years ago, and the grass has come back. This patch is the closest thing we have to a native tall-grass prairie. All four of the tall Texas grasses grow here: big and little bluestem, yellow Indiangrass, and switchgrass. Little bluestem is light green in summer, rich brown and bronze in winter. Big bluestem is called "turkeyfoot" because its three seed heads look like . . . well, turkey feet. The seeds of Indiangrass are yellow-gold, with purple tips, and the leaves are burnished copper in winter. Switchgrass, sometimes higher than my head, has a flyaway seed and a root system that's strong enough to drill through hardpan. There are other natives, as well: sideoats grama, blue grama, wild rye, curly mesquite.

This isn't pure native prairie, though. In places, it's been invaded by alien grasses: tall, vigorous, drought-resistant King Ranch bluestem, from China by way of California; the notorious Johnson grass, from Turkey; Bermuda grass from Africa, seeded in neighboring pastures and carried here by birds and the winds. Hardy and persistent, these introduced species will eventually overtake the native grasses, as they have almost everywhere else. There's precious little native prairie left in Texas; what remains is almost invisible, lying remnant in cemeteries and hidden corners like this one, or in ribbons of railroad right-of-way. Productive, readily exploited, easily invaded, the original twenty million acres of Texas tallgrass prairie has virtually disappeared. Less than 1 percent remains.

It's the same story everywhere across the heart of this country. There's virtually no prairie left. No great loss, some think—it's just grass, after all. They envision "higher and better" uses for the land: annual crops, improved grasses, parking lots, subdivisions. They see a good return on a small investment. But as Wendell Berry says of prairies and virgin forests, it is almost impossible for us now to understand their real value or to measure the worth of our uses of the land. That's because we cannot see the ways we have changed the land from what it was before we entered it. "We came with visions," he says, but not with sight. . . . The prairies could not survive because in their place we saw cornfields and pastures sowed to the cool-season grasses of the Old World. And this habit of assigning a higher value to what might be than to what is has stayed with us, so that we have continued to sacrifice the health of our land and of our own communities to the abstract values of money making and industrialism.

But it's not all gone, not just yet. There are still other natives, here, gladdening the morning. There are the tall, delicate wands of azure sage and ankle-high violet ruellia, sometimes called the prairie petunia. Along the wooded fencerow in summer, I see purple ironweed and square-stemmed, spotted horsemint. And frostweed, which blooms in summer-white clusters atop tall stems. With the first hard freeze, the stems split, squeezing out frozen sap in showy crystalline curls that vanish in the winter sun.

The dogs and I are heading back toward home now, the path snaking through a forest of shrubby sumacs whose lacy, elegant flower clusters summon countless midsummer insects. In September, when the clusters have turned to clumps of dark red berries, raccoons climb the slender trunks, which bend and sometimes break under their weight. White-tailed bucks rub their antlers against the trunks, sometimes rubbing off the bark. Showing their dominance, researchers say. Leaving their marks on the world, a bit of buck graffiti. "This is my place, mine. Mine."

There's cedar here, too, the ubiquitous Ashe juniper. The burros kept this corner clear, but now that they're gone, and in the absence of the natural fires that used to clear this area, the brush is reclaiming it. In another twenty years, these junipers will have grown together into a cedar brake, a place for small animals and birds, a little less space for prairie. It would take several days' hard work with the chain saw and several more days of hauling and burning to clear the corner. And realistically speaking, clearing is only a temporary fix, gaining at best a few years for this tiny scrap of native prairie. Absent fire, all this land will be forested in another three or four decades.

We're nearly home now. There's Bill's workshop, the carport where his old Ferguson tractor lives, the huge old live oak, she-of-ten-trunks whom we call Gaia. There's my garden, and the antique rose bushes along the walk—yes, real antiques, own-root, no hybrids, dating from before the Civil War. There's the old wheelbarrow full of familiar culinary herbs, thyme and sage and parsley and chives, with southernwood and santolina nearby, and the half-barrel where we kept goldfish until a water snake moved in while we were away and ate every one. We wouldn't have solved the mystery if we hadn't found the barrel full of water but empty of fish and the guilty party still present, curled snugly in the bottom, sleeping off his meal. We named him Snorkel (obviously) and released him into the creek.

But there, hanging by the back door, is a rusty cowbell whose mystery we will never solve. What cow wore it? Whose cow was she? How did she lose her bell? Did she drop it? Did she die of old age? Was she killed by Indians, by a mountain lion, by hungry neighbors, by accident? We'll never know. There are lots of things about this land that we will never know.

I think of this often. I think with a kind of awe that no human being has ever made a permanent home on this particular spot on the globe—Bill and I are the first. But that doesn't mean that this place has no history, or that the land has not been used and changed by humans. Its unimaginably long past is written in layers of limestone rock, in tree rings, in the arrow points chipped by Indians passing through, in rusty cowbells and the marks of wagon wheels on rock. Everything has a tongue. Everything speaks.

To hear it, I have to be patient, and still, and silent.

CHAPTER FIVE

Naming

The naming calls. Calling brings close what it calls. . . . Thus it brings the presence of what was previously uncalled into a nearness. . . .

MARTIN HEIDEGGER, *POETRY, LANGUAGE, THOUGHT*

To hear the unembodied call of a place, that numinous voice, one has to wait for it to speak through the harmony of its features—the soughing of the wind across it, its upward reach against a clear night sky, its fragrance after a rain. One must wait for the moment when the thing—the hill, the tarn, the lunette, the kiss tank, the caliche flat, the bajada—ceases to be a thing and becomes something that knows we are there.

BARRY LOPEZ, *HOME GROUND:*
LANGUAGE FOR AN AMERICAN LANDSCAPE

January 20, 1989. Cleared a huge tangle of elbow brush and wild black-berries from Lazarus' Meadow, along the upper bank of Pecan Creek. Lazarus, that ancient mesquite, has finally given up the ghost. Bill is harvesting the last branches for woodturning projects.

December 15, 1992. Finally got title to the strip of land that includes Gaia, the enormous, enormously ancient multi-trunked live oak on the other side of our lane, home to birds, squirrels, raccoons. I can't say why this was so important to us, only that this tree seems to be a symbol of the place, and it feels good to have her under our protection at last.

November 12, 2000. Transplanted six bald cypress seedlings (grown from seed gathered under Claudia, the first of our cypress plantings and now a tall, proud tree) along the intermittent creek that flows out of the lake, which we named Cypress Branch after we bought this part of the property last year. Bill has put up several new bluebird houses along the trail through Cattail Marsh. Saw a male northern harrier while we were working—looked him up later in the field guide and learned that his genus name (Circus) comes from his habit of flying in low circles when he hunts—eyesight eight times better than humans. Also: an osprey over the shallow north end of the lake, dropping down to seize a fish—stooping, as is said of hawks. Also called sea-eagle, fishing eagle. "Osprey" comes from ossifraga, *literally "bone-breaker."*

NAMING OUR PLACE was the first thing we did when we decided to settle at Meadow Knoll. We chose carefully because we aimed to stay for a long time and we wanted a name that meant something to both of us. Meadow Knoll described the fields and gently rolling hills, and although it didn't sound very "Texan" (names like Two-Bar-H, Silver Spur, and Running T are common around here), we liked it.

"We need a richer vocabulary of place," Scott Russell Sanders says, reporting that there are fewer place names per square mile in the United States than in other long-settled countries, where streams and hills, grassy places and even rocks wear a name and tell a story. As Barry Lopez remarks in *Home Ground*, however, the problem may not be that we don't have enough place names, but that we don't know the names given by the native peoples, previous dwellers—names that have been lost as the people and their stories slipped out of sight and out of memory.

Naming connects us to the places that have significance for us, places that tell our stories. How do we know where in the world we are if we can't place ourselves in the landscape? How can we describe a natural setting if we don't have a vocabulary that defines its features? *Savanna*, for instance, to describe the open grasslands here in the Hill Country. Or *motte*, a small clump of trees growing on the savanna: here, usually a clump of live oaks, with juniper and mesquite. Or *caliche*, a hardpan mix of gravel, sand, silt, and clay, cemented together with calcium carbonate, weathered limestone. (This is the stuff underneath my garden. It makes good roads.)

Two people who live and work in an intimate relationship to a place need a vocabulary to specify locations within that place—a map to the territory they share, a functional collection of reference points, a repository of memory. These names don't mean anything to anyone else, but they are meaningful to Bill and me, part of the practical geography of our lives in this place. Just where was that hawk feather found? (Under Lazarus, in Lazarus' Meadow.) Where was it Susan saw the bull snake sunning himself on a rocky ledge? (Beside Iris Pool.) Where is Bill going to cut trees this morning (in case he doesn't come home when he's expected and I have to go look for him)? Where is the fence down? Where are the first cattails showing green? Which bridge across the creek needs repair?

Generally, we name by landmarks, the way native peoples do. The creek that flows along one side of the property, designated merely "intermittent" on the county map, is Pecan Creek, in honor of the pecans along its banks. Cypress Branch flows out of the lake and into Long Pool, which lies at the edge of The Beyond and has been home to striped bass, carp, and sunfish and a pair of snapping turtles named Simon and Schuster (after one of our early publishers). Canyon Falls—a joke, really, since the "falls" are only a foot high—channels the flowing water to Turtle Pool, named for the Red-eared slider who laid her eggs in a hole she'd dug in the bank. Goat Island, where we found the carcass of a neighbor's goat, lies around a bend, downstream. Below Goat Island is Hidden Pool, where Mama Superior and Papa Macho—two of our gray Toulouse geese—liked to make mad, passionate love in the early spring. Rachel's Run flows into the creek between Ripple Run and Crescent Pool, named for its shape. There's a bridge over Iris Pool, where I planted Siberian iris along the marshy edge. Hurst Falls is downstream, named for the friend from whom Bill bought the property, and Cedar Pool, for the ancient cedar that once leaned over the water. Below that, there's a water gap bridged by a poor excuse for a fence, and then the creek flows on through pools and over limestone ledges to its appointment with a neighbor's recently constructed tank, and beyond, to Bear Creek, the San Gabriel River, the Brazos, and the Gulf.

The trees, like the creek, are important landmarks. The most remarkable have Biblical names: Methuselah, the oldest and largest live oak on the place, some three hundred years old; Lazarus, the mesquite that came back from the dead; Shadrack, Meshack, and Abednego, the trio of cedars standing together at the edge of the woodlot. But we wanted to honor other traditions, so the land across the creek is Merlin's Corner, home to Merlin, Arthur, and Guinevere—a live oak, a pecan, and an elm. We gave the name Gaia to the enormous ten-trunked live oak that stands guard beside the lane, and Persephone to the huge pecan tree that burned and then resprouted with seven magnificent trunks. The cypress trees we planted along the creek, now nearing thirty feet tall, bear the names of goddesses from different cultures—Freya, Britomart, Diana, Eurydice—and the name of a friend, Claudia. Rachel Carson is a mulberry, beloved of squirrels and birds, Helen Nearing a substantial oak. Many of the trees bear scars where they have been struck by lightning. And many others were damaged in the ice storm that took place a full decade ago but is still remembered by the holes ripped in the woodlot's woven canopy.

We require paths and paths require names. The grassy trail that skirts the woodlot is Ramses' Road, named for the audacious roadrunners (collectively addressed as Ramses, from their regal headgear) that dash along it, bearing lizards from the creek to the little Ramses in the nest. Ranch Road One, meandering through Longhorn Meadow, is bordered by purple pentstemon, bright yellow square-bud primrose, snow-on-the-prairie, and the staghorn milkweed, whose bitter sap feeds the monarch caterpillar and lends the butterfly a bitter taste that makes it almost predator-proof. Methuselah's Path takes us from the house to the creek, through the Woodlot. Cedar Alley follows Pecan Creek. Willow Trail is a track, passable only in dry summers, through the cattail marsh in Longhorn Meadow. Sumac Loop curls around the east meadow where Dee's burros once lived, through the patch of sumac and past the pigpen and the corral that Rick and Greg built. Bill mows the meadow paths, which are used not only by us and the dogs, but also by deer, coyotes, coons, possums, and armadillos. On damp mornings, I can read their paw and hoof prints.

Larger areas definitely need names. The woodlot has always been just the Woodlot, but beyond that, beside the creek, Lazarus' Meadow belongs to the indomitable Lazarus, several of Bill's most productive pecan trees, and a female yaupon holly whose red berries, like grace notes, brighten the melancholy winter. North Meadow is painted with bluebonnets in April, and Meadow Marsh, a seasonal wetland, brims with spring and summer wildflowers—Indian paintbrush, Indian blanket, brown-eyed Susans, scarlet standing cypress, sunshiny coreopsis, and gentians, an impossibly blue splash of spilled sky. Longhorn Meadow is home-on-the-range to our longhorn cow (Texas) and her calf (Blossom, whose daddy was French, a Limousin, *ooh-la-la*). Sharing the meadow is Mutton, a Barbados sheep. Mutton had four sheepish companions, but the nomads' dogs killed them one murderous weekend, when Bill and I were giving a book talk in Tulsa. Or was it coyotes, or even a mountain lion? There were no witnesses left to tell the tale, only Mutton, and we couldn't get a word out of him.

There is no surer way of belonging to a place than by learning the names of the creatures that share it with you. The first few years we lived here, I spent hours in the woods, in the pastures, at the lake, at the creek. I carried a notebook and field guides wherever I went, teaching myself the names of the plants along the fencerows and creek, the trees in the woodlot, the grasses in the meadow.

I learned how to recognize the differences among grama and bluestem and curly mesquite grass, and where these plants were likely to grow, and what they revealed about the health of the soil. I dug cattails in spring to see if their tubers were edible: they were, but only in the direst circumstance, not because of their taste but because of the time it takes to dig and clean them. I made juice from the mustang grapes that festooned the fences (tart, but just right when it's mixed with the juice of other grapes) and picked the prickly pear cactus pods to eat as a vegetable. The ruby-red prickly pear fruits, called tunas, made a delicious jelly, and so did the sharp-tasting red agarita berries I picked along the lane.

Plants are good for other things, too. I discovered that the Osage orange tree that grew along the fencerows of my childhood also grows at the edge of our woodlot, and that the Plains Indians used its tough, springy wood to manufacture bows and its bark to make an orange dye. My Missouri grandmother chopped up those big chartreuse fruits, large as grapefruit and heavy as cannon balls, and put them in her cupboards as a cockroach repellant. I don't have roaches, but I used the bark to dye some handspun wool yarn a light orange-brown.

I've made other plant dyes, too: yellow-orange, from the coreopsis that grows in Meadow Marsh; green and yellow from goldenrod (depending on which mordant I use); black (well, almost) from mesquite root; and red from cochineal bugs, tiny insects that secrete and hide under a cottony white blanket and feed on the prickly pear cactus. Industriously "farmed" by the people of southern Mexico, cochineal bugs produce a brilliant scarlet dye, the most valuable thing (next to gold and slaves) that the Spaniards found in their New World ventures. They quickly established a monopoly, and cochineal became a major cash crop of Central America.

I found out that mesquite blossoms in April are beloved of bees, who transform the nectar into a delectable golden honey. Thus pollinated, the blossoms produce slender green mesquite beans in June and July. Gathered when green and simmered, the beans produce a juice that can be turned into jelly and wine. Or, dried and ground, they are a nutritious if slightly bitter flour, from which you can make bread and booze. And not just food, but beautiful things, too—the vases and bowls that Bill turns on his lathe from downed, ancient trunks. J. Frank Dobie, a great champion of the mesquite tree, reported this Mexican adage: "With prickly pears alone one can live, but with prickly pears and mesquite beans, a person will get fat." I wouldn't want to live on prickly pear and mesquite beans or earn my pay with cochineal bugs, but my soul is nurtured by the knowledge that this land yields that kind of abundance.

I also learned the names of birds and began keeping a list of the familiar full-time residents—cardinals, chickadees, sparrows, mockingbirds—as well as the seasonal pilgrims who show up with predictable regularity. The ruby-throated hummingbirds arrive from the south in late March and leave by the middle of September. One year, the first hummer arrived before I'd taken down the chickadees' suet log, which during the winter hangs on the same hook as the summertime hummingbird feeder. I had to hurry to make the year's first batch of hummingbird hooch to feed the hungry and reproachful traveler, who clearly expected to find dinner waiting at the end of his northward migration. I love to watch the roadrunners, especially visible during the spring nesting months, racing with beaks full of grasshoppers and dangling lizards to feed their voracious young.

One March afternoon, we witnessed a flock of white pelicans heading north to their summer breeding grounds, flying low, like so many pieces of origami turning and twisting in astonishing unanimity. They landed briefly at the lake, but judging that it wasn't large enough for safe harbor, they flew on. In April, we welcome the purple martins, who sing gleefully, nest in the martin boxes, and depart on a single day in August, en masse. May is nesting time for the bluebirds, who move into the boxes Bill has built (clearly in accordance with their specifications since almost every box produces at least one brood). Throughout the spring, the wrens nest in the handiest nearby container—a flower pot, an empty teakettle, a hanging basket—and shrill their alarm whenever we approach.

One year, a purple finch built a nest in the porch rafters near the busy hummingbird feeders; the fledgling finches watched and learned, then tried to mimic the hummers. It took Mom a little while to persuade them that bugs were their favored food. For years after, purple finches visited the rafters, like family returning for a reunion.

Another year, a great crested flycatcher laid her eggs in a bluebird box on the dead mesquite beside the creek. Much too large for the box, she had to sit with her tail out the door. Her chicks hatched successfully and made their scheduled departures from the nest—all but Tail-end Charlie, who perched in the doorway shrieking for his supper until he was as big as his mother.

In May and June, migrating males arriving for the breeding season put on a spectacle. I watch the male scissor-tailed flycatcher (also called the bird of paradise, for his fine plumage) flying swooping loops and somersaulting dives for his ladylove. I listen for the sweet, tumbling lyrics of the male painted bunting and hope for a sight of his opulent purple, red, and green iridescence, or his shy mate's arresting chartreuse. July arrives with the clatter of the yellow-billed cuckoo, which my mother always called a "rain crow" for the bird's storied habit of heralding a coming rain—not very accurately, west of the Ninety-eighth. His miscues are easily forgiven, though, because this bird—a relative of our other local cuckoo, the roadrunner—has an insatiable appetite for tent caterpillars, ripping the webs apart in search of tasty morsels for his fledgling brood. And all through the summer nights, I can hear the repeated, monotonous call of the poor-will and his cousin, chuck-will's-widow.

In October, Bill and I celebrate the sandhill cranes' annual October fly-overs, on their way south to their winter home along the Gulf: "It's Sandhill Arrival Day!" one of us will shout, having heard the news from on high and spotted the wavering V of the flock's flight, impossibly far above in the crystal sky. The other will hurry out to look and listen to the sandhills' wild, primitive clamor, which fills us with a joy so unspeakable that we can only blink back the tears. November brings the red-breasted robins, arriving at Thanksgiving in a chattering cadre of fifty to a hundred birds, just in time to feast on the ripening rose hips, yaupon holly, and pyracantha berries. In December, the American goldfinch and a variety of warblers show up, along with the towhees and evening grosbeaks, and always the bronze-headed cowbirds, whose piratical practice as a nest parasite I abhor but whose liquid, gurgling song is a delight. How can I love a bird's song and hate her parenting habits with an equal passion?

I am often surprised. I once watched as a half-dozen sociable cedar waxwings lined up on a limb, politely passing a juniper berry back and forth from one end of the line to the other, until one finally took the initiative and swallowed it. Another time, I saw a black-masked loggerhead shrike, inelegantly but descriptively called the butcher bird, as he lived up to his name. He impaled a squirming grasshopper on a mesquite thorn, calmly ate it, then swiped his beak clean on the limb. Later, I found the remains of a locust impaled on a barbwire fence: the shrike's calling card, left as an advertisement to a female shrike to persuade her of his hunting prowess. Still later, I discovered what looked like the pelvic girdle of a tiny frog dangling from a mesquite thorn. Who else but the butcher bird could have left it there?

Family matters. One afternoon, down by the creek, Bill saw two red-tailed hawks mating in a flurry of feathers at the top of a dead mesquite tree; one evening in late December, we shared the binoculars to spy voyeuristically on a pair of great horned owls in the old oak in the south meadow, engaged in the same urgent business. On a warm day in April, we watched a hawk in her nest atop Rachel Carson (a fine mulberry tree), feeding chunks of green snake to her chicks. That evening, I took a photo of them peering curiously at me over the rim of the nest, the lowering sun turning their baby hawk-fuzz into golden halos. The nest was used the next year and the next, until it was destroyed in the ice storm.

On another April day, we watched, entranced, as a Rio Grande turkey hen (we call them, collectively, Thomasina) led her brood of four young poults across the meadow, the smallest repeatedly falling behind and, with a frantic flutter of tiny wings, scrambling to catch up. When the mustang grapes ripened in August, I saw Thomasina and her four youngsters, much larger now, feasting lustily on the purple fruit. In the fall, Bill was working at the creek when he was startled by the rattling buzz of wings and looked up to see her flying just over his head, so near he might have touched her—followed by one young turkey and then another and another, the whole family, all five, still together, taking flight.

There have been infrequent visitors, too. Once a pigeon, gray-green and iridescent purple, a metal band on his leg, appeared on the front porch, obviously exhausted. We called the local pigeon fanciers' group for advice in returning him to his owner and were informed, in a kindly way, that a homing pigeon is perfectly capable of finding his way home without a map or a compass. We fed him the chickens' corn and gave him water. When he was rested, he left on the next leg of his journey. We watched him go and hoped for his safe arrival.

Another drop-in visitor, a white-fronted goose apparently separated from his migrating flock, stayed for some early winter weeks as the not-quite-welcome guest of our own flock of gray Toulouse geese. The visitor, whom we called Grayling, was a handsome bird, but his tremulous, high-pitched *ho-ho-honk* was more diffident than the brash, braying cries of the resident Toulouse and they closed ranks against him. Geese are clubbish birds, and a lone goose is a sad sight. Rejected, Grayling was forlorn and obviously lonely for his own kind. When he flew away, we wished him safe passage, hoping that he was headed south to Port Aransas and Goose Island, where the rest of his white-fronted friends were undoubtedly spending the winter in the warm, welcoming waters along the Texas Riviera.

FOR NEARLY A DECADE, Meadow Knoll had no official address, other than the town and a zip code. People found us by phoning for directions or consulting the map we gave them. The UPS and FedEx delivery people had special instructions on the packages that came our way: "See map in van for directions to Alberts." Eventually, with the advent of the 911 emergency system, we were assigned an address. And now, with the aid of the global positioning satellite, Meadow Knoll's location can be pinpointed from outer space. I am told that Google Earth might even allow people to see me going out to feed the birds or water the garden. Now, that's a thought to conjure with.

But that's a different part of the story. An official address is no substitute for a home for the heart, and while GPS may keep me from getting lost, it will never bring me closer to what is real, what is true, what I need. For that, there are names. "Calling brings close what it calls," Heidegger says, "brings the presence into a nearness."

Naming, we have moved from outsiders to this place to insiders, to an authentic, earned and even (sometimes) unself-conscious sense of where we are, to what Edward Relph calls an "'I-You' relationship with place." We are on a first-name basis with the land and its creatures, all of whom we respect and care for, most of whom we love. We are doing the difficult work of place-making, becoming inhabitants, not quite native yet, perhaps, but somehow kin.

And it is naming that brings me home, here.

Naming, I am closer to what I perceive.

Perceiving and naming, I am nearer to knowing.

And knowing is what I want to do in this solitary place—know the community of this land as fully and deeply and intimately as I can, know who I am, know where I belong.

CHAPTER SIX

All Our Food Is Souls

If you are what you eat and you don't know what you're eating,
do you know who you are?

CLAUDE FISCHLER

All our food is souls.

INUIT SAYING

October 26, 1988. Shredded three heads of cabbage for sauerkraut tonight, using the antique slaw shredder we bought in Nova Scotia. I wonder how old it is— fifty years, a hundred? It's one of those tools that worked so well that there was no need for innovation. I'll brine it for a day or two, then can it. (Read somewhere that during the First World War sauerkraut was called "Liberty cabbage.") Also made some turkey sausage—not as much salt as there is in the commercial sausage. And I know what else is in it, too. No mystery bits in my sausage. Did a quick revision on Bill's section of the Hardy Boys book.

February 2, 1989. Planted a couple of rosemary bushes beside the back door, have a tray of baby basil plants, savory, sage just unfurling their second leaves in the kitchen window. Put the spring broccoli and cabbage plants out a couple of weeks ago, green onions, planted early peas. No point in doing potatoes again—just too hard to make a crop here. My mother says it's not a garden without potatoes, so I guess mine isn't really a garden.

March 17, 1989. Ordered my first batch of chicks, a mixed lot of two dozen layers—looking forward to brown eggs! It's as much fun to read the hatchery catalog and drool over those fabulous chickens as it is to read the seed catalogs and drool over those gorgeous plants. But I won't have to weed the chickens.

September 22, 1989. We wanted geese—today we acquired an entire flock. Toulouse geese, big, gray birds, heavy: a breeding pair, six young geese from this year's hatch, an older goose. The first thing they did was to rush down to the creek to swim in the clean, moving water—their joy was a delight to watch. The second thing they did was to head for the chickens' feeder to get a load of groceries. Their wings are clipped, but by the time their feathers have grown out, they will have figured out that this is their home. We'll let them fly, trusting they'll come back.

IN 1985, I READ *Diet for a Small Planet*, by Frances Moore Lappé. The book, now a classic, gave me an idea of how our American food chain worked and how what I ate affected other life forms. It startled me into an awareness of what I was putting into my body—what it did to me, where it came from, and what it really cost, which is different from what I paid for it. The book exerted an enduring influence over the way I choose foods, cook, and eat, both at home and in restaurants, an influence that was reinforced when I read *Laurel's Kitchen*, with its emphasis on whole foods and homespun recipes that didn't require a lot of fuss and bother.

After I left the university, I discovered that I had fewer social obligations and ate fewer restaurant meals, allowing me to choose a healthier diet. (This was in the mid-1980s, long before healthy eating had become the media topic it is today.) Rice and beans made it to the table much more often, beef and pork less (and less and less, over the years). I indulged in vegetables and fruits, avoided sugar, and substituted herbs for salt. I became interested in organic gardening, sustainable agriculture, and raising my own meat—theoretical interests rather than practicable, because at the time I was living in a condo.

When Bill and I began planning our move to Meadow Knoll, I staked out my garden space, a sunny spot with the best soil on the property. That wasn't saying much, because most of Meadow Knoll is covered by a thin layer of alkaline soil depleted by too many seasons of cotton, eroded through overgrazing, and underlain by a thick limestone shelf that in places is only a few inches below the surface. When Bill rented the backhoe to dig the pit for the septic tank, he kept it an extra day and dug my garden. He helped me build raised beds, and I began the long process of enriching the soil with compost, manure, and grass clippings. (Ah, that homegrown compost, made more fertile by cow manure, kitchen waste, coffee grounds, and our own homegrown, personally produced, nitrogen-rich urine.)

I learned to garden in the rich, deep glacial soils of Illinois, learned it from my mother, Lucille Franklin Webber (born in 1909), who learned it from her mother, Mary Susan Jones Franklin (1881), who learned it from her mother, Sarah Elizabeth Talbert Jones (1859), and her mother, Mary Ann Coldiron Talbert

(1840), who was half Cherokee and could live (Grandma said) as well and easily off the land as out of a garden. In Illinois, we planted potatoes the first of March and dug them before the ground froze in late October. Green onions went in as soon as the soil thawed and were on the table a month later. Peas hung on the vine like dewy green pearls by May, strawberries were lush and ripe by the middle of June, and we were eating sweet corn and watermelon on the Fourth of July. All summer, Mom and I canned bushels of beans, quarts of tomatoes, pecks of pickles. Gardening was a matter of putting the seeds in the ground at the right time, religiously pulling the weeds, and thankfully harvesting the garden's bounty.

Texas was a whole other country. Here on the Ninety-eighth, we have two gardening seasons: February through June (some years) and September through early December (some years). Since rainfall and temperatures vary widely from year to year, it's hard to count on a crop and easy to get discouraged. If I don't have tomatoes by June, forget it—the days are already too hot. The tomatoes blossom, but the plant won't set fruit when the temperature tops ninety. Zucchini, squashes of all sorts, most varieties of beans, sweet potatoes, spring broccoli, and fall carrots and cabbage do well, but potatoes don't—a huge disappointment. Like its nightshade cousins, the tomatoes, the potato doesn't produce its fruit (the tubers) when the soil is too warm. I still hear my mother's voice: "It's not a garden without potatoes."

And then there are the critters, large and small. The raccoons love the corn and are savvy enough to wait until it ripens to strip it from the stalks. They also like beans, cucumbers, zucchini, and all kinds of squash, although when it comes to zucchini, even they can't eat it all. I have a generous spirit when it comes to garden truck, but I'm not willing to share the broccoli with the cutworms (I learned to use paper collars) or the cabbage with the cabbage worms. These are naturally fond of cabbage, but any number of bugs, not so narrow-minded, disdain specialization. Anything green appeals to them, except weeds, of course, which are beneath their notice. Pity. I'd be delighted to share the weeds.

And there is the rain, or rather, the lack of it. I began gardening in Texas in a dry spell, in years when we had fewer than twenty-five inches of rain. Even though it was mulched three and four inches deep with newspapers and grass clippings, the garden demanded a great deal of water. A drip system wouldn't work because of the variations in water pressure, which meant using a spray irrigation system. Because persistent low rainfall meant that the aquifer was low and well recharge slow, pumping became a challenge. I'd run the pump for ten minutes, then run to turn it off for twenty, then run back to turn it on for ten, and so on. All that running was good exercise, but tough on my temper. It cut into the available writing time, too.

After five or six years of laborious and frustrating vegetable gardening, I decided that Webb's thesis about the Ninety-eighth Meridian was accurate: there is a vast difference between the wooded east and the arid west, a difference that can be measured in inches of rain; degrees of June, July, and August temperatures; and the extent of the gardener's patience. I also decided that the old lie was truly a lie: the rain does not follow the plow.

Having come to these conclusions, I rested on my laurels (I really did can a great many beans in those years, and the squash and fall cabbage were splendid) while I revised my gardening scheme. I would grow tomatoes (which Bill doesn't eat) in deck containers, and Bill would grow hot peppers (which I can't eat) in pots. Organically grown vegetables were beginning to appear in the markets, so we would eat those, locally grown whenever possible. I would grow herbs and native perennials and a little of everything else from time to time, just to keep in practice. And I'd keep the compost pile going, because I believe in compost. Decay is one of the few things in life you can count on.

The chickens proved to be far more rewarding, interesting, and entertaining than the vegetables. Bill built a lean-to coop with an adjacent fenced run against the back of our garden shed, and I ordered a couple of dozen chicks from a hatchery in Missouri. They arrived one April morning at the post office in a cardboard box cushioned with excelsior, holes punched in the sides, and Charlie Barton, our postmaster and friend, phoned us at six a.m. to suggest that we come and pick them up. They were peeping, he said, very loudly. He thought they ought to have something to drink. The chicks—strong, healthy balls of yellow chick-fuzz—spent the next few days under a light bulb in a corner of the kitchen, and then moved out to Amazing Grace, who once again proved her resourcefulness and versatility by serving as a brooder house until the chicks graduated to the newly built coop.

My childhood experience of chickens was memorable. On my grandparents' farm, the Sunday dinner menu inevitably featured chicken, fried or stewed with my grandmother's homemade egg-rich noodles. I was commissioned to roll out the noodles, cut them into narrow ribbons, and hang them to dry on a towel draped over the back of a wooden kitchen chair. And I was allowed to go with Grandma to help choose which chicken was next on the list for the stewpot or the skillet.

This was difficult business, for I was inevitably fondest of the very bird Grandma thought should come to dinner with us. The victim selected, next came the execution. The first two or three were eye-openers. Was my mild-mannered, soft-spoken grandmother really going to tackle that savage rooster with fiery eyes and the two-inch spurs? Yes, she was, and I watched open-mouthed as she waded into the flock, snatched him up, and wrung his neck with one deft flick of her wrist.

A few minutes later, the rooster was scalded with boiling water from the tea-kettle and the carcass was mine, to pluck the feathers. I had my first lesson in cleaning a chicken from my grandmother, who showed me how to pull out the innards without getting the inside of the innards all over the outside of the chicken, and all over me. (For most people, this particular skill-set would prove to be of limited value in adulthood, but I certainly put it to good use when I had my own flock.)

At dinner, my grandfather always inquired the identity of the chicken that was making a guest appearance at the table. "Big Tom," my grandmother would say matter-of-factly. "Didn't he stew up nice?" I had to admit that he did, once I recovered from the shock of recognizing that I was a predator. I ate with good appetite, discovering that I was every bit as fond of chicken and noodles as I was of the chickens that ran around the yard in pursuit of grasshoppers and crickets. In that way, I learned early on to make the connection between what lived in the barnyard and what came to the table—a vitally important lesson that is no longer available to most kids. I also learned that if you intended to eat something, it might be better not to give him or her a name. Better to think of it as an "it."

My Midwestern experience with chickens proved a more reliable guide than my Midwestern experience of gardening (chickens can't tell when they've crossed the Ninety-eighth, as long as someone remembers to give them water). Our Texas chickens were energetically, ecstatically free-range, spending their days foraging for bugs in the meadow grass, squabbling over beetles and katy-dids in the fencerows, taking lazy dust baths in the sun under the cedar tree. The Girls—mostly Rhode Island Reds and Buff Orpingtons—were dedicated lay-ers. They gave us more jumbo brown eggs than we could eat, and I sold what was left. (I read recently that eggs from "pastured" hens were going for six dollars a dozen in California. I believe it. They are beyond price.) Chauntacleer, our chief Rooster-In-Charge, carried out his duties with a touching devotion, putting his rooster foot on a squirming grasshopper and *cluck-cluck-clucking* to his harem favorites, summoning them to come and feast on the tasty tidbit he'd caught just for them. At dusk, he rounded up The Girls with great care, counting heads and tails, making sure that none were left outside the coop when dusk fell and owls and coons were on the prowl, lured by the rich, ripe scent of chicken.

That was the laying flock, which we enlarged by the simple expedient, every now and again, of giving one of the hens a half-dozen eggs to hatch or putting a batch of fertile eggs (candled, to make sure) into the incubator. The table flock was different. Every spring, I ordered four dozen Cornish Cross chicks from the hatchery, stuffed them with high-protein feed for six weeks, and butchered them. Since I'd never mastered my grandmother's flip-of-the-wrist technique, Bill employed his axe while I boiled water to loosen the feathers and prepared to clean, cut up, package, and freeze the birds. Four dozen chickens, each dressing out at more than five pounds, would feed the two of us until the following spring, when it was time to order more.

Bill and I weren't trying to live independently of the supermarket or attempting to be self-sustaining. We simply believed that producing some of the food for our table, as long as we could do that efficiently and enjoyably, was the right thing to do. One year, we bought a young steer that had been raised on the grass of a nearby ranch without chemical inputs and without being fed the "finishing" diet that makes beef fatty. His tasty meat filled the freezer and (double wrapped, carefully bagged) gave us all the beef we needed for several years: a hundred and thirty pounds of steaks; a hundred and fifty pounds of ground beef, stew meat, and soup bones; a hundred pounds of roasts; fifteen pounds of brisket; and the liver, heart, and tongue—not one ounce of it permeated with antibiotics or growth hormones.

In other years, we bought young 4-H pigs and fed them to table-size, without antibiotics or growth-promoting hormones. The first one, Big Red, was lazy, and he'd just as soon lie in a muddy corner as eat a good meal. But Big Pink was something else again. A sizable fellow to start with, he had a remarkable appetite. That pig lived to eat. From dawn to dark, we'd hear the sharp rattle-bang-clank of the mechanical door of his feeder and know that this porker was doing his piggy best to live well and prosper. Big Pink, whose photograph was displayed on our refrigerator for years, was an unquestioned success. His hams were superb, his chops were spectacular, and his bountiful bacon had *not* been cured with nitrates.

Perhaps you are frowning as you read this, finding it heartless, even brutal, to eat animals with whom one has shared a personal history—animals that have been named, fed, nurtured, and, yes, even loved, as much as an educated, well-read, well-traveled, adult American woman can love a pig. But that's exactly the point. Most of us buy our meat in hermetically sealed packages out of the meat cases in the supermarket, making no connection between what is in the package or on the plate and the living, breathing, feeling animal whose life has been taken—often brutally, inhumanely, and unsanitarily—so we can have meat. (Whether Americans need all the animal protein and fat we consume is quite another question. The obesity epidemic suggests that we do not.)

As a responsible omnivore, I need to know where my food comes from and understand and respect the needs of the fellow creatures whose deaths make my life possible. The chickens that gave us eggs and went into the freezer were treated with care and concern; they had the run of the meadows, with all the green grass and grasshoppers they could eat. The calf was born and raised on a ranch, in freedom, not on a factory farm. The pigs kept their tails (the tails of pigs raised under close-quarter stress are docked to prevent chewing), lived comfortably in a sizable pen, bedded in clean straw, and had lunch whenever they felt like it. What's more, all these animals came from this place, or nearby. They shared the soil with us, the water, the weather, the air. In that, there is a certain deep integrity, a wholeness, a relationship, which I find richly satisfying.

I also found it much more satisfying to cook food that I had raised. And since we had chosen to live an hour's round trip from the nearest fast food and more than that from a good restaurant, we ate almost exclusively at home—as we still do, dining out only a couple of times a month. (Someday, some researcher is going to discover that people who live more than twenty miles from fast food restaurants are healthier and live longer lives.) I learned to cook out of the garden, in season, or out of the freezer, or out of the canning jar. I made bread and a deliciously yeasty pizza dough and jelly and jam. I made up my own recipes for mustard and sausage and pickled peppers and cheese and crackers—yes, even crackers, which are great fun to make and much more various than anything you can buy. I have taken a perverse sort of pleasure in handcrafting the products that have for so long come "prepared" from the supermarket that we have forgotten how to make them ourselves.

Bill and I learned these things for ourselves in the 1980s and 1990s, through experimentation and trial and error, all part of a personal philosophy of food and diet. We still eat our own produce as much as we can. But now, I am heartened to discover, the practice has a name—"ethical eating"—and the foods that I made in my small kitchen are now called "artisanal" foods: handmade, unbranded, personalized breads, crackers, cheeses, mustards, pickles, and jellies, all produced by real people (artisans, at that), not machines.

There is even a movement—the "slow food" movement—designed to promote traditional culinary habits and home cooking and discourage drive-through dining. And yet another movement—the "eat local" movement—has grown up in response to globe-girdling supply chains. It aims to shorten the distance between farmer and fork and make us aware of the true cost of food that is shipped halfway around the world before it arrives on our tables. "Locavores" calculate "food miles" and advocate consuming mostly food that is grown within a couple of hours' travel of home. (Big Pink and the table flock would certainly qualify.) These interests have been encouraged by several books, among them *The Omnivore's Dilemma*, by Michael Pollan, and *Animal, Vegetable, Miracle: A Year of Food Life*, Barbara Kingsolver's memoir documenting her family's determination to live off the land for a year. Good efforts, I think, important efforts. I read this kind of work with respect, admiration, and a (I trust forgivable) sense of been-there-done-that. And the unsettling sense that a future of depleting energy resources may require each one of us, all of us, to roll up our sleeves and garden.

There are difficulties, of course, at least for me. Growing all your own vegetables west of the Ninety-eighth is truly an unpredictable business, which is why Barbara Kingsolver moved from Arizona to Virginia to conduct her experiment of living on the land. It takes more time and more water (in most years) than I can easily come up with. There's also the interruption of necessary travel. My grandparents rarely left their farm and were always available to feed and water their animals, but being at home 24/7 has become a serious challenge for Bill and me in the past few years. It is nearly impossible (as any farmer will tell you) to find someone to look after your flocks and fields while you are visiting bookstores and going to writing conferences—although as the years go on and energy costs increase, perhaps we won't be traveling so much.

All of this means that producing our food is no longer the intense hands-on, do-it-yourself practice it was during the first decade of our life here. But what I gained during that time will remain with me for the rest of my life—and not just a conscious awareness of my food, either. I have become acutely aware of all that I consume: household supplies, clothing, furnishings, electricity, gasoline. Where does it come from? Who made it? What's it made of? How long will it last? How can I use it most wisely? And especially, what is its true cost (in fossil fuels, fossil water, environmental impact, as well as dollars)? But food remains at the top of the list, and as I write this—with gasoline topping four dollars a gallon and the words "peak oil production" hitting the news, I have the feeling it will stay there.

As the Inuit say, all our food is souls. We are what we eat. Yes, it is so, and literally.

It behooves me, then, to know what and whom I am eating, and what kind of life they lived before they became me.

THERE WERE OTHER animals with whom we simply shared our place, without inviting them to the table. We kept bees until the Africanized bees appeared on the scene and we thought it prudent to leave beekeeping to those who could tell the difference. For a few years, we had a small flock of pearl guineas, inherited from Robbie when we bought his property. They were noisy creatures with an opinion about everything, always delivered in sharp, staccato bursts, like impatient machine guns. In contrast, the Muscovy ducks, Tofu and Yogurt, were voiceless, offering up only an urgent hiss when they had something to say.

The black ducks we bought at the feed store were sold as mallards but proved to be Indian runners, ducks that can run so fast that they are used to train sheep dogs. The insufferable drakes teased and tormented our female geese until we took them to Indian Wells Lake and released them. They were home in thirty minutes. Determined, we drove them twenty-five miles west to Lake Buchanan, bade them Godspeed and released them into the wild. We were afraid they might beat us home, but happily, we never saw them again.

The three white Pekin ducks—Moby Duck and his two hens, Quacker Oats and Creamy Wheat—were a different story. We grew very fond of Moby, who listed heavily to the right due to a regrettable tangle with a piece of wire netting when he was a duckling. Moby demonstrated a tender affection for his ladies and a strong sense of responsibility for their welfare. In fact, he died in their service, defending them, in their pen, from an attacking raccoon. Bill shot the coon, and we buried Moby beside the creek where he loved to paddle. His ladies, heartless, transferred their affections to one of the geese.

Ah, those geese, those geese! The flock came to us as a family, nine Toulouse geese: Papa Macho, Mama Superior, Auntie Em, and six of Papa and Mama's spring hatch. Toulouse are large birds, up to thirty pounds, with gray back and wing feathers, gray necks and heads, white bellies, orange bills and legs. Handsome and stately, they moved with an admirable dignity and sense of purpose. Their wings were clipped when the flock came to live with us, but when they acquired their new flight feathers, they flew with evident delight around the lake and back home.

Sadly, flight was Auntie Em's downfall. She caught a strong north tailwind one stormy afternoon, misjudged the height of the electrical wires over the driveway, flew into them and broke her neck, falling dead at my feet. While we did not intend to eat these birds, I thought it would be a pity to waste such a large, healthy goose. I put her into the pressure cooker, which turned out to be a good thing. Auntie Em had been around for a while, and she was more muscle than meat. But it was good meat.

Mama and Papa, impassioned lovers and experienced parents, produced five or six goslings a year, most of whom we gave or traded away. (We laughed that we were populating Burnet County with Toulouse geese—it was probably no joke.) Mama laid a great many eggs, sometimes as many as thirty in a season. I made off with them before the snakes and coons found them, then put back six or seven for her to hatch. The others were mine, all mine, and a treasure. I poked holes in both ends and blew out the whites and the yolks. One goose egg (four times the size of a chicken egg) makes a delicious omelet for two, folded over a filling of cheese, mushrooms, fresh dill and parsley, chopped green onions. I used the empty shells to make *pysanky*: intricately decorated Ukrainian Easter eggs created by painting layers of wax over layers of dyed color, then melting the wax over a candle flame to reveal the brilliant patterns. Mama died some years ago, but I still have a box of her eggs stored in the closet, ready to be transformed into *pysanky*—when I get a little time.

In spite of my best efforts at family planning, however, the goose flock grew. Each year, we kept a couple of goslings, and they produced their own offspring. Henry, our neighbor's massively dewlapped Toulouse, walked over to our house one morning and liked the company so much that she stayed. (Her eggs were even larger than Mama's.) Someone gave us an African goose we named Duchess, who imperiously refused to share the wading pool we filled for the geese when the creek was dry. Fed up with her haughty ways, we traded Duchess and her favorite gander, White Wing, to some friends, in return for a peacock.

And so began another chapter in the barnyard saga. We named the peacock Picasso. He was a gorgeous, strutting bird with a jeweled fan of a tail that he displayed with energy and exuberance to his peahen, to the chickens, to the geese, to Moby and his ladies, to me—to anything that moved. Sweet Pea, his mate, was a modest, mild-tempered brown bird of maternal bent. She obviously found Picasso enormously attractive, for they hadn't been together for more than a couple of hours before they were planning the next generation.

The peachicks came along faster than we could name them: Peoria, Petunia, Peabody, Pansy, Pablo, Paisley, Prentiss, et al. Less amenable to penning than the chickens, ducks, and geese, the peafowl roosted in trees at the edge of the woodlot, where one night Picasso lost half his tail to a greedy raccoon who set his sights on the whole bird but had to settle for a mouthful of feathers. Sweet Pea preferred to hide her nests, but we usually managed to find them: one in a patch of tansy (a smart choice, we said, because tansy is an insect repellent), another in the tall grass behind Amazing Grace, another in the field (not such a smart choice, apparently—a snake or a coon got the whole lot). When I could, I took the extra eggs. They made interesting *pysanky*, too.

The peachicks were funny and charming and the adult peafowl were entertaining, but they all wanted to be top bird and felt compelled to outshout the competition. They screeched when Bill ran his chain saw, when the rooster crowed, when a train whistled, when a plane flew overhead. And since their cry sounds remarkably like a woman in fear of her life, a muster of peafowl can sound a lot like murder. They liked to sit on the front porch railing, where at any given moment, you could find three or four, discussing the weather or the availability of grasshoppers, and (of course) pooping, ever and always pooping. Their proximity presented another problem, too: when the phone rang, the peafowl screeched, to the point where we had to shut the windows and doors in order to talk. This occasioned some interesting comments from our New York agent and editors, who got the idea that we were very weird people—an idea that was reinforced one day when I had to abruptly drop a phone call to chase Robbie's cow out of my garden.

The porch was a popular gathering place for all the barnyard fowl, which meant that it had to be washed daily. Picasso liked to sleep on the roof, which got him into real trouble one cold February morning when he woke to discover that his tail was frozen to the porch roof under a sheet of inch-thick ice. His indignant squawking woke me (Bill had conveniently gone to Houston), and I went out in the predawn chill and saw what had happened. I thawed him out by spraying him with the hose (our water, which comes from four hundred feet underground, is about seventy-two degrees year-round). With some effort, he managed to pull loose and fly to the ground. Except that it wasn't a flight, it was a belly flop. His tail was still frozen in a chunk of ice and the poor bird never really got airborne. Picasso dragged the ice around behind him until afternoon, when the sun finally melted it.

One thing about barnyard fowl is that they are powerfully, magnetically attractive to predators—everything from coyotes and foxes to raccoons, skunks, and snakes. The foxes and coyotes usually kept their distance, but the coons, skunks, and snakes were out in force most nights. We live-trapped coons (praying we wouldn't inadvertently trap a skunk), loaded them into the truck, and drove them off to a creek some miles away, where we released them—not a good solution, but better than shooting them.

The snakes were an entirely different matter. It's impossible to fence out a snake: Bill once watched a substantial fellow skinny himself to the diameter of a rope in order to slip through the mesh of chicken wire. They squeezed through cracks, crawled underneath floors, slid down the roof, curled around the rafters. They dined on chicken eggs, duck eggs, goose eggs, and peahen eggs, whatever was on the menu at that particular season. Of course, this is all part of Nature's Grand Plan, and it is true that most of our snakes are nonpoisonous. But I never failed to look before I put my hand into a nest to take an egg—*my* egg. I designed the coop, Bill built it, and we paid for the chicken feed. I can be forgiven for insisting on being Top Predator.

And it wasn't just eggs those snakes were after, either. Early one morning, when Sweet Pea and her little brood were roosting on the fence around the compost pile, I caught a bull snake in the act of swallowing a whole peachick, headfirst. The snake was promptly dispatched, but the chick was a goner. And late one night we heard Papa Macho squawking furiously, ran out to the goose pen, and found that a bull snake had swallowed one of Mama Superior's large goose eggs (the telltale bulge in his belly clearly incriminated him) and was in the act of gulping another. Bill killed the snake, retrieved the still-whole egg, and returned it to Mama. In the due course of time, she hatched it. We named the gosling Jonah.

Snakes are also agile tree climbers. One spring afternoon, we heard the frantic chattering of a squirrel and witnessed a ferocious mother defending her nest of squirrel babies high in a hackberry tree. Head down, clinging to the tree trunk with her hind paws, she had grasped the attacking snake in her forepaws and was swinging him from side to side, forcing him to loosen his grip on the tree. She finally pulled him loose and dropped him to the ground where he landed with an audible thud. Our cat, OJ, ran out to investigate. We followed, arriving in time to see a bull snake, chagrined, slither drunkenly away, wondering what had hit him. If you don't believe me, I understand. I wouldn't have believed it either, if I hadn't seen it for myself.

Meadow Knoll is home to a wide variety of snakes: bull snakes, rat snakes, hognose snakes, green snakes, whip snakes, ribbon snakes, and racers, all non-poisonous. But we have the other variety as well. Bill killed a fifty-two inch rattlesnake in our dog's water bowl one night when the dog quite properly refused to go into his run, and we happened on a cottonmouth near the creek. Around here, it's a good idea to watch where you put your feet.

Life with a yard full of barnyard fowl is full of many different kinds of excitements, from proud announcements of eggs to frantic warnings of predators, from the *cluck-cluck-CLUCK* that signals a juicy grasshopper to the raucous goose-gabble and peacock shrieks that herald the arrival of a FedEx delivery. But the writing changed, and our lives changed, and we had to find new homes for our friends. If I could, I'd love to have chickens again, and ducks and certainly geese.

But maybe not peacocks.

CHAPTER SEVEN

Gaining, Losing

Things as they are, from a human perspective, requires an acute appreciation of loss—total loss, loss of self and loss of world. This is what freedom means. This is the real shape of the sacredness of the world, the union we find within the particularity of each moment of our lives.

NORMAN FISCHER, "THE SACRED AND THE LOST"

December 12, 1994. Computer problems. Looks like we'll have to get a new machine. This old one just isn't fast enough to handle the desktop publishing I'm doing now. How many computers have we gone through in the nearly ten years we've been married? I've lost count—but I'll bet they're all still around here, some-where. Bill has trouble throwing anything away (we might NEED it someday), and we're running out of storage space fast.

January 17, 1995. Just back from Danville, after a week with Mom. Things aren't so good there—hated to leave her. Since Dad died, she's managed very well for herself, but that's coming to an end now. It's hard for her to get around, and somebody has to shop for her. She needs more care at home—help with baths and dressing, help with meals—but who can do it?

March 12, 1995. Bad news. Mom fell and fractured her pelvis. Bill's driving up to get her and bring her here—the nursing home in Bertram is a nice place, and only fifteen minutes from our house. I can't even think of having her in a nursing home in Illinois and driving eighteen hours (one way) to see her. And now we're going to have to close out her house and sell it. Oh, lord.

July 1, 1995. House shopping. There's no room to work here, let alone room to have a life. And I'm running out of shelf space for books. We obviously have to do something.

FIVE ACRES AND SAMMY and the cabin for tool storage and Grace for odd jobs (brooding the chickens and serving as a craft shop and meditation room)—that was the beginning of it, and for several years this was sufficient for our residence and work and recreation. As our activities broadened and we could afford it, we acquired outbuildings: the garden shed for the tools we used to work around the place; Bill's woodworking shop and a couple of carports; the chicken coop; and a metal building that we called the Library, storage for books and other necessities that we weren't using but weren't ready to dispose of (the stuff normal people stow in their normal basements, attics, and garages).

But by early 1995, Sammy simply wasn't big enough for all our activities. We began to collect house plans, survey possible building sites at Meadow Knoll, and discuss our finances. We were already committed to a small-is-beautiful philosophy when it came to housing; after all, we'd been living for nearly eight years in 696 square feet. What would it cost to build a modest house, say, around 1,200 square feet? Who would build it, and how much of the work could we, would we do ourselves? How would we fit all this into what was an already crowded calendar and still do the writing that brought us our living? We looked at the bank balance and looked again—could we acquire a new house without acquiring a mortgage? (In those pre-sub-prime days, banks rightly considered writing a risky occupation.)

Already, 1995 had been a year of losses. In March, my eighty-five-year-old mother, happy and independent in her Illinois home, fractured her pelvis. We brought her to Texas to recuperate in the locally owned, family-oriented Bertram Nursing Home. Mother settled in and, with her characteristic cheerfulness, made herself at home. I loved having her nearby: she had been part of my life for more than half a century, and it was good to be close. Perhaps, if she grew well enough, she could live with us—in Sammy, if we built another place for ourselves.

But first we had to clear out her house and sell it, a painful job made more difficult by the distance, the summer's heat, and the stress of having more work to do than two people, working hard, could reasonably manage. Bill's parents were not in good health, and he was making frequent trips to Houston. And we were up against deadlines. By that time, we were working on two adult mystery series and both of us were busy with other writing-related work. We needed more space, we needed it urgently, and we didn't have an extra minute to give to the project. When Bill asked me what kind of house I wanted, I heard myself say "an instant house."

That was when we began looking at plans for manufactured homes. When we found one we liked, Bill phoned the Texas builder and discovered that there was a model on a lot in Dallas. As it happened, we had to go to Dallas for a book conference that weekend, and our route took us right past that lot on I-35. It was an auspicious sign.

But things got even better. We loved the real house as much as we had loved its floor plan, and the model—the one we had first admired in the catalog—was for sale. In fact, because all the homes on this particular lot had to be moved to make room for a Wal-Mart (some cosmic irony at play here?), we could have it at a giveaway price: $35,000 cash, which included settling the house at Meadow Knoll. Within two weeks, our new dwelling arrived, mortgage-free, towed by a pair of large tractor trucks in lieu of a yoke of oxen.

And that's how we got Serenity. In his usual methodical way, Bill staked out the spot where the new house would best fit into our landscape, with attention to the views from the windows and connections to our existing utilities (septic, gas, electricity, phone). It was a simple house but twice Sammy's size, with a generous master bedroom-bath, an office for Bill and a writing studio for me, and (glory!) three large walk-in closets, in addition to the usual kitchen-laundry, dining-living room. With added front porch, back deck, and corner fireplace, Serenity is even more comfortable now. The front windows look out across the wide meadow to the cedar-studded hills on the other side of our neighbor's creek. My studio window gives me a view of redbuds and daffodils in spring, wildflowers in summer and autumn, and deer year-round.

There were other gains in the next few years, giving us more elbow room. We bought our neighbor Robbie's property, which included a complete (more or less) perimeter fence and interior fences, in addition to a well, a tool shop, and a pole barn, as well as a furnished but never-lived-in single-wide with a view of the lake. We named it Tranquility Base—perfect for a getaway place and guest house. Not long after, Dee sold us nine more acres, including the pasture that had been home to the burros, an impenetrable cedar brake, another well, a corral stout enough to restrain a buffalo, and several tons of rusted metal junk, including the rear end of a trailer truck and a thousand-gallon tank that had once contained oil (and still did, although what was left looked like tar). The junk has gone to the scrap-yard, the pasture has since returned to pre-burro health, and the well irrigates our pecan trees.

Ah, yes, the pecan trees. A couple of years after we settled in, Bill grafted Desirable and Choctaw scions onto twenty young wild pecans, growing randomly where floods and squirrels had planted them. He went on grafting each spring, adding Kiowas and more Choctaws, until he'd successfully grafted some forty trees. Managing them takes hours of spraying, fertilizing, and hauling irrigation hose, but the effort's worth is measured in pecan pies and snack nuts. The latest crop weighed in at some two hundred pounds (more pies than are good for us), and the yields will increase through the life of the trees, more than eighty years. They'll be here, delighting squirrels, jays, and humans with their October crop, long after we're gone.

We got our first dog in 1992, a mixed breed stray with one blue eye and one brown. We named him Val because he arrived on our doorstep on Valentine's Day. We lost him four years later when he developed severe hip dysplasia and had to be put down, but we soon gained another dog, our black Lab Zach, who became a constant friend. A rescue dog, Zach was joined a few years later by Lady, another rescued black Lab with an extraordinary sweetness of demeanor who lived with us until her death not long ago. Toro wasn't a rescue but rather a volunteer; a blue heeler with a compelling desire to keep everybody on task, he bounced into our lives on Bill's birthday, on the same wild November day that a tornado skipped past us, about five miles to the south. We lost our beloved cats OJ and PK to old age and our white cat, Gorby, to a predator. But a replacement arrived shortly (how do they *know*?): Shadow, a black cat who loves Bill's lap.

In the mid-90s, faced with the need for more frequent book-related travel, we gave away or sold our chickens, geese, and peafowl. Feeling the loss, we acquired an elderly longhorn cow named Texas and her last calf, Blossom, to whom we assigned the task of mowing the upper meadows, a duty they perform with unending enthusiasm and a 24/7 dedication. They keep company with Mutton, the lone survivor of the Barbados flock we lost to predators.

There were more important losses in those years. Bill's brother, David, a forest ranger, died at his home in Alaska. His father, Carl, a dear man whom we loved deeply, died in 1999. My mother never got well enough to come to live with us. She died in July 2000—a graceful death that she chose for herself by the simple expedient of deciding not to eat.

Over the sixty-year span of our relationship, Mother and I had been alternately close and distant, I plagued with the conscious awareness that I was not a good-enough daughter—not attentive enough, not understanding, not sympathetic; she always hoping that we would have something like the warm relationship she had with her mother. But my mother and grandmother shared the same fundamental understanding of what women were supposed to do and be, what daughters were supposed to learn from mothers, and I was on the other side of a profound divide, generations away, a continent apart, light years distant.

My favorite photograph of my mother shows her in her late twenties, her brown hair marcelled in the style of those days. She has a delicate face, with wide cheekbones and a sweet mouth, and her expression is eager, optimistic, almost wistful. She could not be blamed if some of that eager wistfulness was worn away by the stark difficulty of living with my father, and optimism was tempered by realism. But she never lost her cheerfulness, and in her last years, I came to admire her patient, willing, almost Buddha-like acceptance of her age and infirmities, and to think, *That's how I'd like to face death, when it comes to me.* We were not mother and daughter, then, but two human beings holding on to each other and then letting go, for that's what death is, a last long letting-go into the dark.

Sometimes I think that lessons in holding on and letting go are the most important things I've learned in this place. The solstices and equinoxes come and go, the springs and summers and winters pass in a predictable procession. We celebrate the arrival of seasonal visitors—birds, butterflies, animals, wild-flowers—and hope for their coming another year. Plants grow, become mature, and die. Companion animals bless us with their presence for the span of their lives; we treasure each day they are with us and mourn deeply when we must say good-bye. Family, friends, dear ones—how do we count the losses when we must let them go?

But let them go we must, let them all go—the birds, the animals, the people. "By June our brook's run out of song and speed," Robert Frost says in his poem, "Hyla Brook." The peepers are silent, the jewelweed broken and bent, the stream itself vanished with the summer heat, "a brook to none but who remember long." Still, in the light of presence or the shadow of loss, in the ebb and flow of having and losing, in the whole telling of what has been and gone and is no more, we love.

And we remember long.

CHAPTER EIGHT

Right Livelihood

I am a competent but essentially invisible writer, proof that one can earn a living from writing for years without ever breaking into the public consciousness. That's okay, or so I've always claimed: all I ever wanted was to write, quietly, for a living. Who knows what monstrosities of ambition lie buried in that assertion?

JOHN JEROME, *THE WRITING TRADE:
A YEAR IN THE LIFE*

November 11, 1988. Saw Heart of Danger *(one of my Nancy Drew books) in the bookstore yesterday. Just a little book, but it pleases me to know I wrote it. Also have a new project for MegaBooks, another one in the* Sweet Valley Twins *series. In the works as well, the outline for* Extra! #5, *with Bill—so there's plenty of writing work, which keeps the bottom line more or less healthy. Wish I had a little more enthusiasm for it. But at least I'm working at home, which remains the highest priority.*

September 14, 1990. Great news! Work of Her Own *is going to Jeremy Tarcher, for their Fall 1992 list. Couldn't ask for anything better than that. And since the manuscript is already finished—just a few odd bits to be tidied up—I've told Bill I'm going to tackle that murder mystery I've been thinking about, the one with the garden theme.*

November 26, 1991. Totally blown away. Scribner's has offered for Thyme of Death. *And not just for the first book, but for the whole series package, three books. And since* Thyme *is finished, they're ready to put it out—hardcover!—in October '92. China Bayles is on her way!*

January 11, 1993. Looks like the Victorian series is going to Avon, under the pseudonym of Robin Paige. Paperback original, which is a disappointment, since we wanted hardcover. But it's a place to start. Bill is very happy about this new development—I think he'd almost given up hope that we'd be writing together again, after we stopped doing the young adult work. And we've moved the China Bayles series from Scribner's to Berkley, with Natalee Rosenstein, which pleases both of us.

April 23, 1997. Writing From Life *just arrived—a real book at last, a very long time in the making. When did I start collecting material for this? About the time I finished* Work of Her Own, *wasn't it? I'm always struck by the time it takes for an idea to take words, get into print, between covers. This cover is beautiful. Love it.*

May 27, 2002. Natalee has agreed to do the "family mystery" series— The Cottage Tales of Beatrix Potter, *it's called. I'm pleased to be working with the Potter material—fascinating character, lovely period of history, wonderful setting. A nice change of pace from the other two series.*

BY THE TIME BILL AND I were settled at Meadow Knoll, we were already fairly confident that we could support ourselves with the work-for-hire writing we were doing, books for children and young adults. Over the next five or six years we would write more than sixty of these books—so many, in fact, that Bill called us the "book-a-month club."

As writing jobs go, these were interesting and enjoyable enough. We were invisible writers, yes, never writing under our own names, but who cared? The work required less in the way of research and rewriting than magazine pieces and was much more dependable. Most of the books in these series were published on a monthly schedule, and editors tended to call on reliable writers who met their deadlines and whose work needed little revision. Once we began to work with an editor, we could expect more assignments to come our way. I learned a great deal during these years about the craft of fiction and the business of working for editors and publishers of mass-market books. I also learned about the value of discipline, planning, and sheer tenacious plug-headedness. And still more about the art of writing with another person, which may be hardest of all to master, especially since that person was my husband.

It was not all work-for-hire. By 1988, Bill and I were pitching our own ideas to editors. We sold several novels to a German publisher (written in English for translation into German), and in 1988–1989, we sold and wrote (yes, that's the right order—selling the project happens before it's written) the first six books in a projected series called *Extra!*, set around a high school newspaper. It was an appealing project and we had high hopes for it. But the publishing house, a start-up, went bankrupt when a warehouse company failed. This sort of thing happens occasionally in the business, leaving writers, editors, and publishers stranded. You learn to take your lumps.

This kind of work was interesting, yes, and mostly enjoyable, but best of all, it fit the description of "right livelihood," a Buddhist concept that had become very important to me. Right livelihood involves working in an occupation that calls forth the best in you, encourages you to grow, and enables you to respect yourself while you respect the needs of people and of the natural world. Writing for a living (with the exception of writing advertising copy, maybe, or bomb-making instructions or pornography) meets that description, as far as I'm concerned. And writing is a right livelihood that I can successfully pursue at home. What more could I want?

But as the 1980s drew to a close, I began to feel I had outgrown the young adult work and to think about putting my writing skills to work in a more satisfying way. I decided to write a book about the experience of career-leaving, based on my own experience of leaving the university but broadened to include other women who had left positions of leadership and authority to build new lives outside the career culture. The project sold to Jeremy Tarcher, and *Work of Her Own* was published in 1992. In 1997, Tarcher published my second nonfiction book, for women interested in journaling and memoir: *Writing From Life: Telling the Soul's Story.*

Neither of these books was a blockbuster, but each led to something more important. When I was writing *Work*, I interviewed a couple of women lawyers who were running from the law. Those interviews led to the idea for a mystery series featuring a woman who leaves a successful career as a criminal defense attorney to find her own right livelihood, becoming an herbalist in a small Texas town. In 1997, *Writing From Life* led to the creation of a strong group of women writers, the Story Circle Network, a nonprofit organization with an international membership that continues to flourish. My life was enormously changed by both these projects. I like that about writing: you can't write without learning, and you can't learn without growing, so in that sense, every writing project changes me.

I enjoy the challenge of writing nonfiction, but I am a storyteller above all else. My father, a voracious reader, introduced me to the classic mystery writers, storytellers all: Dorothy L. Sayers, Agatha Christie, Ngaio Marsh, Patricia Wentworth, Rex Stout, John D. McDonald, Dashiell Hammett. Never very deeply interested in American noir (crime novels featuring tough, cynical men and fragile or evil women), I was glad when women writers began to develop the female private eye character, beginning with P. D. James' *An Unsuitable Job for a Woman* (1972) and continuing with the entries of Marcia Muller, Sara Paretsky, and Sue Grafton into the field in the early 1980s.

These popular successes persuaded publishers that readers were interested in women's mysteries, and the end of the 1980s not only saw the creation of popular amateur sleuths by Carolyn Hart, Nancy Pickard, and Margaret Maron, but also the establishment of Sisters in Crime, an organization for writers and readers of women's crime fiction. The next few years also brought an increasing interest in regional detective novels with strong female characters, and writers like Sharyn McCrumb (who writes about Appalachia), Dana Stabenow

(Alaska), Joan Hess (Arkansas), and Nevada Barr (national parks around the country) got their start. Mysteries are traditionally written in series, so once an author finds an audience and becomes established, she can usually count on continuing publication—no small comfort in the risky business of writing for a living.

Carolyn Hart, Sue Grafton, Marcia Muller—they were the company I wanted to keep. Writing for adults seemed a greater challenge than writing for young people, and if I could develop a protagonist and a setting that readers enjoyed, I thought writing mysteries could be at least as dependable as work-on-assignment. Of course, I had absolutely no right to think this, and I would have been justly served if my hubris—these "monstrosities of ambition," as John Jerome calls them—had resulted in a fine fall.

I've always liked mysteries. I like the fact that, unlike many literary novels, mysteries have a strong plot with a beginning, a middle, and an end (preferably a surprising end in which the hitherto concealed truth is fully revealed). I find it satisfying that the acts characters commit have significant moral consequences, change other character's lives in demonstrable ways, and result in some sort of justice, whether administered on the spot or in a court of law. I like the idea of writing about women characters, primarily for women readers. And I very much like the idea that writing books in a series enables a writer to develop a continuing relationship with readers.

That was how the China Bayles mysteries began. I wrote the first, *Thyme of Death*, on time that was paid for by the advance for *Work of Her Own*, which was finished before the contract finally came through. *Thyme of Death* features a former criminal attorney who has bailed out of her career and moved to Pecan Springs, Texas, to open an herb shop. I had encountered herbs in my mother's garden, learned about them in my graduate work in Medieval Studies (medicinal herbs appear in many manuscripts), grown them in the gardens at Meadow Knoll, and even made herb wreaths for sale at a shop in Austin—a shop not unlike China Bayles' fictional Thyme and Seasons Herb Shop. Creating a character who worked with herbs was just another step in the development of my fascination with the "useful plants."

It took a while for my agent—a woman I had met through *Work of Her Own*—to sell the project. The complete manuscript and the series proposal, together with outlines for the second and third books, went the rounds of the New York publishing houses, collecting one rejection after another (encouraging rejections, but rejections all the same). At last, in one of those weird quirks of fate that almost makes me believe in the Tooth Fairy, the package landed on the desk of Susanne Kirk at Scribner's. She recognized Pecan Springs as a fictionalization of a Texas town (San Marcos) where a member of her family had lived and she had visited, and she offered for the book forthwith. My father was dead by that time, but I remember thinking that he (never impressed by anything I had done, not even my hard-won PhD) might have been impressed that his daughter's book was being published by Scribner's. But probably not.

The Tooth Fairy, in her literary incarnation, continued her good work. A few months later, Natalee Rosenstein, at Berkley Prime Crime, bought the paperback rights, and *Thyme of Death* was nominated for both an Agatha and an Anthony (awards given by writers and readers in the mystery community). By that time, the second book was finished, the third well begun, and translation and large-print rights had been sold. With the fourth book, we moved the series from Scribner's to Berkley's new Prime Crime line, under Natalee Rosenstein's wing, where we have been ever since. As I write this, I have just finished the seventeenth book in the series.

When the China Bayles project made it into print, Bill suggested that we write an adult mystery series together. We tried out dozens of ideas until we settled at last on one that both of us were enthusiastic about: a series of historical mysteries set near the turn of the century in England. The mysteries would feature husband and wife amateur sleuths and a slew of well-known real people: Conan Doyle, Beatrix Potter, Rudyard Kipling, Lillie Langtry, Winston Churchill and his mother Jennie, Consuelo Vanderbilt Marlborough, and so on. Bill had traveled widely in England, knew the lay of the land, and had friends there; I loved Victorian novels and thought I had a sense of the way people talked and dressed and lived their lives. The mysteries, which appeared under the pseudonym of Robin Paige, were a pleasure to write. Each was different and required more and different research, so that after a time we had happily collected a couple of hundred books about Victorian-Edwardian England and made several trips to England to travel to the sites of our stories. But the research requirements were as daunting as the work was interesting, and there were other things we wanted to do. We had originally intended to write ten Robin Paige books; we wrote twelve before we closed the series with a mystery about Guglielmo Marconi, set in 1903.

The second book in the Robin Paige series featured Beatrix Potter, the author and illustrator of *The Tale of Peter Rabbit* and other children's books. Reading about Potter's life, I found her to be such a fascinating woman that I decided to use her as a protagonist in a family-focused series set in the English Lake District, where Potter bought a farm in 1905. *The Cottage Tales of Beatrix*

Potter began with the 2004 publication of *The Tale of Hill Top Farm*. The eight books—each a mystery, all featuring Potter's animal friends and the residents of the village of Near Sawrey—cover the years between 1905, when she bought Hill Top Farm, and 1913, when she married her country lawyer, Willie Heelis.

Back in the old days, when I was doing work for hire, all I had to do was finish the manuscript, send it off, revise as instructed, and cash the check. The kind of writing I'm doing now involves a great deal of after-production work: marketing, marketing, and more marketing. The writer's life has not always been thus. Jane Austen never went on a book tour, or put together a brochure advertising her work, or handed out bookmarks. But modern writers, particularly writers of mysteries and romances, invest heavily in marketing: "shameless promotion for brazen hussies," as the women's organization, Sisters in Crime, puts it. Shameless or brazen, marketing is a necessary fact of the writing life.

And now, with the Internet, there's an even greater emphasis on promotion. Writers are encouraged (in some cases expected) to create and maintain Web sites, send e-letters, blog, and maintain MySpace or Facebook pages. Writers also do bookstore signings, give library talks, go to conferences, and generally make an effort to flaunt themselves, sometimes with the financial backing of their publishing house, usually not. If you like that sort of thing, well and good. If you don't, tough titties—you do it anyway. Without promotion, your book may not be read. And if this one's not read, the next one won't be published. That's the bottom line.

Writing is also a business, which many writers learn to their distress when they find their lives littered with royalty statements and contracts they can't read and agents who don't return their calls. We have had agents from time to time, but an agent isn't necessary when you're staying put at one publishing house, as we have done. We've worked unagented for nearly a decade.

Not having an agent pushes a lot of paperwork onto Bill's desk. He goes carefully through each contract, checks the royalty statements, and stays on top of the various rights issues. All of this requires letters, e-mails, phone calls, faxes, and a filing system, even though he is trying his damnedest to create a paperless office.

Writers belong to the ranks of the self-employed, which means that we're responsible for obtaining our own health insurance, making our own Social Security and quarterly income tax payments, and keeping on top of the frequently changing tax code—as well as managing the irregular cash flows, the periods of drought and abundance, that writers have to live with. (Picture yourself receiving two or three salary checks a year, and you'll understand the size of the challenge.) I am enduringly grateful to Bill for assuming the administrative side of our business and for doing it well.

It is heroic work, although he thinks it sometimes qualifies as wrong livelihood.

WRITING PAYS THE BILLS, but it is not the only work that goes on at Meadow Knoll. Sometimes with my help, more often alone, Bill builds chicken coops, pump houses, porches, and decks; reshingles roofs, reroofs porches, repairs stairs, and rehangs doors; maintains more than a mile of fence; and tends the road. He whacks brush, cuts trees and tree limbs (sometimes twenty-five feet above the ground) with a variety of wicked-looking chain saws; occasionally mows a couple of acres that might in an urban environment be called a lawn; and burns whatever can't be composted whenever the county lifts the burning ban long enough to get the job done. He fixes the pumps when the fire ants short out the electrical connections, maintains the water lines to the stock tanks, and splits the wood for the fireplace. Oh, and cleans the chimney, too.

Good work requires good tools, and keeping them sharp, clean, and organized is a job in itself. And since many of the jobs require power equipment, Bill maintains those, too—as many as thirty gasoline engines, ranging in size from Amazing Grace's V8 motor, the ranch truck, and our two road vehicles, down to the toy-sized engine on my garden tiller. We couldn't live on this place if it were not for his care and attention. And we couldn't handle the writing if he didn't keep the computers, printers, faxes, and other electronic equipment running—no small task in itself.

We often laugh at our naiveté when we remember that one of our goals when we moved to Meadow Knoll was simplifying our lives. When you live in town and something goes wrong, you call the appropriate repairman, or raise Cain with the city utility department, or hire a lawyer. Out here, you learn for yourself how to do what needs to be done, and eventually you get pretty good at it. You acquire the right tools. And you learn to use them the right way, without cutting off your thumbs.

But in other, more important ways, our lives really are simpler. We can choose to work or play as the spirit moves us (although writing is so much like play that I can almost not tell the difference). We don't spend hours stuck in commuting traffic—in fact, we rarely go to Austin more than once a month. We don't lose ourselves in the bread and circuses of the mall or the movies, and we go out to dinner only when we really want to, not because we're bored.

And it's not just a matter of going out or staying home. We live a life of chosen solitude here, away from noise not our own, from outdoor lights at night, from the stress of competitive coworkers and supervisors. For more than twenty years, our comparative isolation at the end of an unimproved road, with no neighbors' houses that we can see, has allowed us to enjoy a sweet and precious privacy. We don't think of ourselves as reclusive or antisocial; we stay connected with family and friends and see people when we choose. I'm privileged to share my life with someone I love, but when Bill's not here, for a day, a night, a week, a month, I'm not lonely. I've learned to cherish whatever time I have by myself.

Perhaps it's because living here, together, has taught me how to be alone.

CHAPTER NINE

Alone, Together, Apart

I hold this to be the highest task of a bond between two people: that each should stand guard over the solitude of the other. For, if it lies in the nature of indifference and of the crowd to recognize no solitude, then love and friendship are there for the purpose of continually providing the opportunity for solitude. And only those are the true sharings which rhythmically interrupt periods of deep isolation.

RAINER MARIA RILKE, *LETTERS TO A YOUNG POET*

July 11, 1987. Bill's gone to Houston for a couple of days, so I have the place to myself—cool, lovely mornings, long afternoons, quiet evenings, no sound but birds, the wind, the slight noise made by my pen across the paper. I'm learning that it's not my husband's absence I look forward to. It's the enlarged presence of every-thing around me when I am alone—and especially when I'm alone out here.

December 28, 1988. One of the things I've learned in the two-plus years of this increasingly intimate marriage is that there are limits to intimacy. No matter how close I am to Bill, how much I depend on him, or how much I love him, I am irrevocably and ultimately alone in the world. And the only way I can be fully in touch with myself is to have some time apart from him. There seem to be two forces working within me, urgent, uncomfortably contradictory: to be connected and to be separate.

September 22, 1989. Inks Lake campground. Getting away by myself for a couple of days—a break in the routine, but more than that, time alone, not time to work, just be. It's lovely here—the breeze off the lake is cool and the ducks are a joy to watch. But the campground is noisy. Maybe I should have looked for something more remote. It's not enough just to be away from home. I need to be away from other people, and other people's kids and their boom boxes.

July 17, 1991. Just back from a remarkable four days alone and silent at Lebh Shomea. Remembering Rilke: "Your solitude will be a home for you, and there you will find all your ways." Yes. I've found what I was looking for. There.

OVER THE YEARS of living here, away from the calls and clamors of city life, Bill and I have grown together, overlapped, become a couple, a team, a pair. I look at the books we have written together, the place we have built together, the land we have stewarded together, and think, yes, this is a true joint venture, a strong partnership.

Yet, much of the time we are together, we are alone, individual, not a *both* but an *each*. We may be in the same house together, the same room, the same bed, but Bill is within his body, his mind, I within mine. Walking in the woods, working in the garden, doing a job, talking, embracing—we are together, but we are alone. We're conscious of the other's presence, feelings, actions, but we've gone within, focused, concentrating on what is self, not other. One may speak briefly, the other listen and reply, connecting. And then back to being alone, together.

This didn't happen overnight. Sammy was a small space for two active, mature (most of the time) adults to share twenty-four hours a day, seven days a week, fifty-two weeks a year, year in and year out. Serenity isn't that much larger. While most adults have separate jobs outside the home and spend ten or twelve hours of the day apart, we not only eat and sleep together, but work and live in each other's laps. It has been a crash course in intimacy, a practicum in marriage.

There was a steep learning curve involved with this in the beginning, as you might guess. And it wasn't just the mechanics of living and working together, hard as that was. Things were complicated by the family baggage that each of us brought: his family, his brothers and parents; my family, my parents and brother; and my children and grandchildren. Adrift on the seas of these occasionally stormy affiliations, it could be difficult to separate my feelings from Bill's, his from mine. When he was feeling low and sad, I was blue. When I was angry, he tasted the bitterness. When one of us was frustrated, the other shared it, not in a good way, and our frustrations smacked us against each other like unmoored ships, wave-tossed. Sometimes hard words were said, sometimes tempers frayed and snapped. We've had to learn to resist this almost irresistible tendency to crawl inside each other's skins and stay there, parasitic wasps inside a host. We've had to learn to separate, or we wouldn't have stayed married long.

But there's more to it than that. We were in our forties when we married, and each of us already had a personal history of needing time alone. I had married early and raised three children; at midlife, I wanted the intimacy and companionship of marriage but not at the expense of solitude. Bill had lived alone all his adult life and loved solitary travel. He once spent three months driving alone across Canada in a 1950 Chevy pickup; he wandered through South America by himself; he took a two-month solitary walkabout across Australia, New Zealand, Tahiti, Fiji.

Being alone became vitally important in the early months and years of our relationship; twenty-some years later, it's even more important. Bill often finds his apartness by working outside—occupied with his tools, his tasks; I find the same solitude in my writing studio, in the garden, in the company of plants and insects and birds. I walk the dogs in the morning; he walks them at night. Sometimes we simply make separate trips to Austin, to do necessary shopping, to go to the library, just to go, to get away for a little while. Time alone in the car is fine time.

Whether it's an hour or a day or a week or a month, we have found that the absence of one of us is a necessary part of being together. This is true for everyone, isn't it? When we are constantly with other people, even those we love (sometimes especially with those we love), we give away chunks of ourselves, until sometimes there's nothing left. And when we are constantly with other people—at work, at play, in the various organizations to which most of us belong we present to the world an artificial self, a constructed image of self, what Carl Jung called the "persona," designed to meet others' expectations of us, to keep the people around us from finding out who we really are.

And there's the rub. When I hand out pieces of myself like candy, or hide behind an inauthentic, constructed image of self, I'm in trouble. What I need is to be whole and wholly myself, complete, authentic, and real.

Being alone gives me back myself. When I'm alone, apart, I'm not tempted to construct the self I think others would like to see. I can listen to myself and what's inside and around me. And listening—whether I'm listening through journaling, serious reading, silent meditation, or simply renewing my wonderment at the world—has become my most important spiritual practice.

For of all the things I have learned out here in the country, away from the city, apart from all the busy-ness and distractions of the career culture, the most important is that there is another Susan hidden within, a self that is nurtured in silence and solitude but holds herself back, perhaps baffled, perhaps over-whelmed, from the frantic treasure hunt that is life out there. This Susan is separate from the disciplined, industrious, dutiful, and desirous selves that col-lectively manage my daily life, do the household work, write books, meet dead-lines, talk to readers' groups, take care of the gardens and the animals, eat and sleep and blog and make love. These selves are wonderful, and I'm not knocking them. I am fond of them and grateful for the way they work together and for their dedication to the roles they play. Thanks to them, I am physically well and as happy in my work and my marriage as anybody has a right to hope.

But there's that other Susan, who contributes to my well-being and happi-ness in very important ways, but who doesn't ask for (and never gets) any atten-tion. She needs to be fed by something else, and as the years moved along and the work of establishing Meadow Knoll and the excitement of the writing career began to settle down, I became more aware of her need for silence, solitude, a place apart.

This awareness was not terribly urgent or uncomfortable. It wasn't a deep, powerful feeling of inner void, or a gnawing sense of letdown or profound dis-satisfaction or discontent or disorientation—nothing like the pitch-black abyss of the "dark night of the soul" through which some people struggle. Perhaps it might have been easier if I had been frantic or desperate, if I had been com-pelled to set off on a spiritual quest to find the thing, whatever it was, that I was lacking. I wasn't searching for a spiritual community, or even for God, for I had come to share the Buddhist understanding that the sacred is within me, not out there somewhere, divine arms folded, tapping the divine toe and waiting with divine impatience for me to quit dawdling and get on the right road to salvation. We are our own refuge, the Buddha says, our own destination, our own author-ity. Our job is to find ourselves, and the sacred within.

I became seriously interested in Eastern spirituality, particularly in Bud-dhism, after I escaped from the known landscape of the university but before I met Bill. I studied vipassana meditation: paying disciplined, mindful atten-tion to what is within and without. Vipassana is a secular practice, very simple, little more than sitting (on a cushion, a bench, or a chair) paying sustained and spacious attention to breath, to feelings, to thoughts, to the complex processes that are going on inside us at each moment, and again and again and always to breath. Paying attention without trying to decide whether this is good and that is bad, only that it *is*. Recognizing it, naming it, letting it go. No blame, as the I Ching says, no judging. "A moment of recognition of judgmental mind is a mo-ment of freedom and wisdom," Stephen Levine says.

What? No judgments? Well, not exactly. If I find myself judging, well, there it is, that's what I'm doing, that's me, that's what I do. Judging again. So I recognize the judgment, name it ("judging"), and let it go. But still, no-judging is tough for someone with a naturally judgmental mind, who has been trained and credentialed in the hard-nosed discipline of literary criticism, where judging is the name of the game.

The physical act of sitting proved to be even tougher. I have a great deal of energy—a blessing when it comes to action, but hard to manage when I need to be still. For months, for a year, sitting meditation was a squirmy hell of interminable twitchiness, a dozen snakes burrowing under my skin. But I figured I could either learn to sit with snakes or not sit at all. So I learned, and gradually the snakes learned, too, and we all got quiet together. Enlightenment seemed an impossible goal, but quiet was something I might just learn to manage.

Sitting meditation—by myself and at the Buddhist Center in South Austin, close to where I lived at the time—was the centerpiece of this practice, but only part of it. Walking meditation, measuring my breath by my footsteps, was a way of taking my snakes on the road. And there was reading, of course. My natural way of learning something is to read everything I can find, so that's what I did, amassing a substantial library in the process. I took classes when I could, and attended lectures and discussions, and embraced the Buddhist idea that my whole life was my course of study, and that if I didn't learn these lessons, I'd get an incomplete and have to sign up for my life again, starting from scratch, confronted by the same old miserable lessons all over again. I also got better about paying attention and listening. I learned to appreciate the clarity of Buddhist philosophy, with its wise distinctions between having and being, its firm renunciation of a materialist culture, its emphasis on living an authentic life, a life whose meaning arises from within, not from without.

I was drawn to these ideas in ways I have never been drawn to the Christian doctrines that were painfully kneaded into me during a childhood of Sunday school and church and Bible reading. Theologies based in promises of heaven and threats of hell only inspired my disbelief, and instinctively, I felt I'd much rather "awaken" than be "saved." I understood why when I read Thich Nhat Hanh's description of that enlightened moment: "The moment of awakening is marked by an outburst of laughter . . . the laughter of one who, after having painfully searched for something for a long time, finds it one morning in the pocket of his coat." I'm not sure about the "outburst of laughter," but I could definitely roll my eyes and manage a rueful chuckle. Hey—there you are, and there you've been, all along, in my pocket.

But finding something you've been looking for on Saturday does not necessarily mean you'll find it again the following Monday—or that you'll even remember to look. You find, you lose, you find again. You awaken, you take a nap, you go out for pizza and a movie, you awaken again. It's a gradual process, and there's always another pocket, another awakening. I awakened to just enough of the truth to recognize a potentially healthy relationship when I slipped into it, so I chose Bill. I was awake enough to choose moving to Meadow Knoll over continuing to live in the city and awake enough to choose a right livelihood over a wrong one.

But when Bill and I married and began the challenging business of living together and finding a right livelihood and making Meadow Knoll our home, I more or less stopped being mindful and reflective and just got on with getting a life. Sometimes, just going on is enough. Sometimes it's all you can do—or at least, it was all I had the strength and the wisdom to do.

For me, it goes something like this: I work on getting my act together, more or less, and when my act and I have reached a certain point, I'm able to shift my attention from "how am I doing?" to "what does it mean?" (Of course, the ideal is to be always mindful of meaning, but that's a little much to ask of most of us, most of the time. Too much to ask of myself, anyway.)

After we had been married and had lived at Meadow Knoll for several years, I began to feel the need for time to reflect and the silence and solitude within which to do it. I went back to the pockets. I taught several courses on silence and solitude for the Jung Society. (Teaching is always, for me, the most intense and personal way to learn something for myself.) I began to seek teachers and read Buddhist texts again—by this time, American Buddhism had become more mainstream and there was more to read—as well as books about mysticism and prayer and the interior life. I got up early in the morning and went out to Amazing Grace and sat in meditation as the sun arose. I began to notice that my practice was extending itself throughout the day, with patches of mindful *being* scattered here and there, among the stretches of mindless *doing* and *having*. I began to notice myself listening more intently, more attentively. Not often enough, but sometimes.

Listening, listening. How else can I be in touch with what is inside me, with what Buddhists call the "suchness" of myself, my true, truest, most enduring nature, beneath and beyond the external presentations of self? How else can I find clarity and meaning? And how can I—how can anyone?—listen to what is inside me unless I can be still? Still enough to listen. Still enough to hear.

This kind of listening is deeply allied to the Christian idea of the contemplative life. I was drawn to what David Steindl-Rast, a Benedictine monk, says about his monastic community:

> The monastery is . . . a place where one learns to keep one's eyes and ears open. "Listen!" is the first word of St. Benedict's Rule for Monasteries, and another keyword is "consider!"—literally meaning to lay your course by the stars. St. Benedict, the patriarch of Western monks, wants them to live *apertis oculis* and *attonitis auribus*, with open eyes, and with ears so alert that the silence of God's presence sounds like thunder.

And so I began to want something like an extension of my quiet, solitary mornings in Amazing Grace, a place where I could listen, could consider. I wanted to step outside of my ordinary life for a time, find a place away from distractions, and keep my eyes and ears open. I wanted a place where there was enough discipline and structure to ground me, but where I would have the freedom of doing nothing more than reading and writing and sitting, if that was what I needed to do, and no aim other than to *listen*. Listen and consider, *apertis oculis, attonitis auribus.*

Well. This was a tall order. I hadn't a clue how to go about finding such a place, or what it would look like when I found it. There was no writer's retreat nearby, and I wasn't sure that was what I was looking for, anyway. A spa certainly wasn't the answer (good grief!). Campgrounds were busy and noisy and full of distractions. I didn't want to do yoga all day or engage in group activities. I spent a wonderful week at the Lama Foundation, a Buddhist retreat in the mountains north of Taos, New Mexico, but Lama was an impractical fifteen-hour drive. If I wanted to be entirely alone, to be where I could look and listen, read and write without being distracted by the sweet dailiness of home, where could I go?

And then I found my way to Lebh Shomea.

CHAPTER TEN

Lebh Shomea

Getting Here, Alone

Give your servant *lebh shomea* (a listening heart)
so as to be able to discern.

1 KINGS 3:9

July 9, 1991. Lebh Shomea. Father Kelly Nemeck shows me through the Big House, then to my room on the second floor, part of a suite, Sarita Kenedy's suite, he tells me. A sitting room with a fireplace (no fire today!), a wood floor, a bathroom with a tub, a high-ceilinged bedroom with red painted tiles and tall, white-shuttered windows all around, facing onto the veranda—chairs, nesting swallows, a cooling breeze from the Gulf. View from the desk in front of the window: a sweep of green lawn, palm trees, oaks and pines, the chapel through the trees. The only sound: rushing wind and the chatter of birds, clear and bright, like water rippling over pebbles. Sweet, sweet sounds in the silence.

December 19, 1991. Maybe the important thing to recognize (again, for I already understand this) is that I don't know where I'm going and I don't know what I want or need.

June 6, 1992. A jay stabbing the dawn with a swift, rapier-like whistle. A hot night, got to sleep around ten. Turned the fan off because I wanted to hear the night sounds, the owl's song and the staccato barks and long glissandos of the coyotes. Coming to this place, slowing down, narrowing my focus to what's now and here, I see how much energy I spin out to no purpose, in entertainment, simply passive submission to stuff coming in that occupies the silent spaces in my mind. Better the silence than all that meaningless noise.

GETTING FROM MEADOW KNOLL to Lebh Shomea requires about five hours of driving, south down U.S. 183 and across the Gulf coastal plains to Refugio, then south on U.S. 77, looping around Corpus Christi. Then still farther south through Kingsville to the village of Sarita, named by John Gregory Kenedy—Don Gregorio, son of the founder of the vast La Parra Ranch—for his daughter. It is a pretty trip on this softly overcast, misty day in late May, across land that is green and gently rolling. I'm in no particular hurry, and I don't have to consult a map. I've been coming to Lebh Shomea—a silent retreat community in South Texas—for twelve years now, and the drive is only the first movement in what I hope will be another tranquil symphony of days in this green island of silence and solitude.

It wasn't always tranquil, though. The land has always been the story here: what's on it (or under it), who has it, who wants it, who can hang onto it. Since the 1880s, the place where I'm headed belonged to the Kenedy family, to Mifflin Kenedy and the dynasty he hoped to found at La Parra Ranch. In the 1940s, the land came to the last of the Kenedys, to Sarita Kenedy East, and a part of it now belongs to Lebh Shomea. The story of the land—which is also the story of the Kenedys and a story of conflict—has framed the visits I've been making here since the early 1990s. It's one of the many fascinations that continue to draw me to this silent wilderness, to the Wild Horse Desert, where I come to listen. Listen to the land, listen to myself, listen to the Sacred.

I'M DRIVING DOWN ROUTE 77, which slices through the vast Kenedy and King Ranches that make up most of Kenedy County. The county itself is enormous, about fourteen hundred square miles, but with only nine miles of paved roads, excluding Route 77, and a population (in 2005) of only 417 people. A little more than four hundred people, nine miles of paved roads, in a county not much smaller than the state of Rhode Island. If you're seeking solitude, Kenedy County is the place to find it.

The village of Sarita is small (half the county's population) and easy to miss, but I know it's here—I've spotted the green sign and the water tower, off to the right. I signal for a left, stop, then turn east off Route 77 at the blinking yellow light. The road once ended at a barbwire fence right about here, for the Kings and Kenedys were not especially keen on a highway bisecting their ranch-lands. If you wanted to go south to Harlingen, say, you turned around here and drove back north five miles to Riviera, then twenty-three miles west to Falfurrias, forty-six miles south to Edinburg, and twenty-three miles back east again, truly the long way around.

But in 1937, the Kenedys and Kings agreed to allow U.S. 77 to slice through their ranches, all the way south to Harlingen and then Brownsville. When the ribbon was cut during Christmas week of 1940, there was a great celebration all over South Texas: brass bands, a rodeo, performing elephants, free food, and a special Christmas vespers, giving thanks for the miracle. Even *Time* was on hand to describe the titanic launch. "The road is valuable—it links ten deepwater harbors in Texas—but all this enthusiasm was not evoked merely because 46 miles of highway had been moved 23 miles nearer the water. Texans celebrated because they now had a right of way through land previously barred to Texans."

That's it. That's the story, in a nutshell. The new highway wasn't just a highway, it was a public thoroughfare across a vast private land—*Los Llanos Mesteños*, the Wild Horse Desert—that had been claimed, closed, and confined behind barbwire fences for almost three-quarters of a century. People immediately drove up and down the new highway, just because they *could*.

But while Route 77 has become the most convenient route for all commercial trucking from Houston to the border, it also imports trouble. The U.S. Border Patrol immigration checkpoint at Sarita is one of the busiest in the country. In one recent bust, agents seized ten thousand pounds of marijuana and, in another, pulled three-quarters of a million dollars' worth of cocaine out of a Chevy pickup. Routinely, Mexican nationals are found hidden in trailers, trucks, cars, vehicles of all descriptions. They are nomads, people passing through, as wayfarers for tens of centuries have migrated north and south along this coast and inland, up the river valleys into the Hill Country where I live, and beyond.

Only now, some of these nomads are illegal. Illegal aliens.

I'M LEGAL, and I head east on a narrow asphalt road between fields of grass and brush toward Lebh Shomea House of Prayer, a gift from the Sarita for whom the town is named. In her will, she bequeathed this remote, unpeopled wedge of land to the Missionary Oblates of Mary Immaculate. These circuit-riding priests, known to the people of the Wild Horse Desert as the Cavalry of Christ, had been bringing the faith to the faithful in this region since the 1850s.

Six miles east of the highway, Lebh Shomea occupies the former headquarters of La Parra Ranch, named for the abundant wild red grapes, mustang grapes, that grow in the area. The road there, this road along which I'm driving, is two-thirds of the county's inventory of paved roads.

I open the car window and smell salt in the misty air—Baffin Bay, an inlet on the Gulf of Mexico, is just off over there, to the east. There are puddles along the road; it's rained here, heavily, perhaps an inch or more of the county's annual twenty-six inches of rainfall. What I see around me is grassy savanna—sea-coast bluestem, cordgrass, and marsh millet—flanked by encroaching masses of scrubby mesquite, huisache, and thorny shrubs, and post oak and live oak trees. The land is flat, very flat.

A couple of miles farther on, my way is blocked by a gate across the road. A man comes with a clipboard, and I tell him who I am. He consults his list, finds my name, and makes a note of my license plate number. The gate to La Parra Ranch—a closed compound that includes the property belonging to Lebh Shomea—swings open.

I drive another two miles through a thicket of palmetto and green mesquite trees. Ahead, at a fork in the road, stands a tall wooden cross with clumps of Our Lord's Candle—yucca—blooming waxy white at its foot. The left fork goes to the working section of the old ranch, which combines ranching with hunting and birding leases. The right fork goes to Lebh Shomea, which occupies the former ranch headquarters and the surrounding thousand acres.

A contemplative community, a place for prayer, Lebh Shomea is perfectly at home in this wilderness. "Guests who share our desert silence for indefinite periods are welcome year 'round," the community's Web site says. "With the exception of meals and the Celebration of the Eucharist each day, there is no predetermined schedule, no imposed structure, only the freedom and creativity of solitude."[3]

I take the right fork and drive on, thinking about the significance of the cross that stands at the crossroads, happy at the beckoning prospect of the free-dom and creativity of solitude, of silent days, long stretches of hours with nothing to do but what I choose, when I choose. It's been hectic at home—meeting a writing deadline, planning a book tour, dealing with a couple of urgent family issues, making sure that Bill has what he needs from me to hold the fort while I'm gone, organizing myself to get away. But all that hurly-burly is past, and I feel the sweet quietness of this place already beginning to wrap itself around me, holding me close. "Silence is God's first language," wrote Thomas Keating, "and everything else is a poor translation." The silence of Lebh Shomea seems to me to have a special quality, a sacred quality, although perhaps all silence is sacred, once we understand that it is not empty, but rich and beckoning and full of meaning.

With the silence comes a slower pace, and I stop to allow several deer, in no hurry at all, to cross the road. On the left is the Chapel of the Little Children, built of terra-cotta-colored block, with wildflowers blooming bright in the misty rain. On the right, a little farther on, a large white stucco garage and laundry once housed a machine shop and vehicle repair. Still farther is the building where Sarita Kenedy East parked her Cadillac. Now, it's a greenhouse. There's not a soul in sight.

The mist is becoming real rain, and I have the feeling that it's raining just for me, a blessing on my visit. I park the car, drape my yellow poncho over my head and walk down a palm-lined path to the back entry of the three-story *Casa Grande*, the Big House, built by Sarita's father after the First World War. The construction took several years, the building materials coming by barge down the Laguna Madre from Corpus Christi to a wharf on Baffin Bay or by railroad to Sarita, where they were loaded onto oxcarts and hauled here. The building was substantially finished by 1923.

At an elevation of thirty-eight feet above sea level, *La Casa Grande* stands on the highest point—a sand dune—of this flat coastal plain. Designed in a blend of Mexican Colonial and French pre-Revolutionary style, the fortress-like building (some ten thousand square feet) replaced the original ranch house, which was moved two hundred yards to the east, where it still stands. The move took a month to accomplish and was said to have required two hundred oxen and mules, far more than it took to move the little village of Bertram, back home. When the house was in place, Sarita's brother Johnny and his wife Elena moved into it. Sarita and her husband Arthur moved into the Big House with her mother and father, taking the north side of the second floor. Sarita, who loved the ranch, assumed its management as her father grew older, while her brother, it's said, was more interested in hunting and having fun.

The Big House has a red tile roof, windows set into arched frames, colonnades, and curvilinear parapets capped by stone coping. There's a lookout tower on the roof where a Gatling gun protected the ranch headquarters from the rustlers and bandits who prowled this wild place in the 1920s. The eastern side of the house is faced with porticoed verandas on the first and second floors. If there's a breeze from the Gulf, some fifteen miles to the east, you can catch it there, on the veranda. I know, for the first time I visited Lebh Shomea, in the early 1990s, I stayed in Sarita's suite on the second floor. That was in July, and the

Lebh Shomea
HOUSE OF PRAYER

LA PARRA RANCH · TEXAS
www.lebhshomea.org

not to scale

heat was sweltering, but the bedroom has wide windows and a door onto the veranda and was pleasantly cool.

The Big House is home to Lebh Shomea's library, the basement kitchen and dining hall, and ten bedrooms and baths. Now, in early afternoon, it is empty-seeming and very still, so still that I am startled by the sharp slap of the screen door closing behind me. The Rule here is silence throughout the week, with a shared few words as a formal part of morning Mass and an hour's lunchtime conversation on Sunday. Silence is what most people come for, what I look forward to most of all.

On the message board in the basement dining room, I find my name on a folded slip of paper. It's a brief note of welcome from Sister Maria Meister, with my room assignment. I'll be in Ezekiel, one of the seventeen dwellings (the word preferred here to "cottages") scattered among the mesquite and palm trees: ten for solitary occupancy, five for dual occupancy, two hermitages. I smile, for I've stayed in Ezekiel before and have fond memories of the deer grazing peaceably just outside the window. Out of curiosity, I check the board on the other wall to see how many people are here just now. Eight, it appears, with some due to leave in a few days, others to arrive. Lebh Shomea can house twenty-five guests, but however many there are at meals and Mass, the silence always remains the same, pure and sweet, the first language of God—or whatever name you give to the Sacred.

I get my suitcase from the car. There's also a plastic crate full of books and writing supplies, a reading lamp, my meditation bench, a bag of knitting, and my laptop (no e-mail or Internet access, but I can use it for journaling). Too much stuff, but less than I intended to bring. I left a box of books at home.

Still, it takes two trips to carry everything to Ezekiel, a small, spare, square dwelling built of the same dark terra-cotta blocks as the new chapel and surrounded by large oleanders blooming pink and lavender. There's a screened-in porch; a white-painted sleeping-and-study room with two windows; a meditation room with a chair, a window, and a cross on the wall; a large walk-in closet with deep shelves along one side; a bathroom with a shower and an on-demand hot water heater. White plastic blinds screen the windows. A long, wide shelf attached to the wall is a perfect desk, with bookshelves above. The narrow bed opposite is neatly made, an extra blanket folded with precision at the foot. The windows gleam, the white vinyl tile floor shines, everything is clean, clean, very clean. There is no clutter. Why can't I keep my house like this?

And then I look out the window and there they are, on the other side of the oleander, so close I can almost touch them—a pair of white-tailed does with four young fawns, still wearing their spots. The misty rain is a silvery sheen across their backs. A doe raises her head, fixes her brown eyes on me with placid curiosity, and slowly, slowly, goes back to the business of cropping grass. Nearby, a dozen wild turkeys drift silently across the lawn, true to their own purposes, their own plans. None show any fear. Lebh Shomea is a wildlife refuge, and the deer and the turkey belong here.

So do I, I think with a long sigh, and the silence, like a prayer shawl, settles across my shoulders.

AN HOUR LATER, I waken, groggy, and for a moment am not sure where I am. I've taken off my watch, but there's a clock on the shelf over the desk. Four-thirty in the afternoon. At home, Bill is feeding the dogs and finishing the day's chores before he makes supper for himself. I feel a quick, sharp stab of regret, of guilt. It was raining when I left, and the forecast predicted more rain and possible flooding, which always make for more work. Bill is doing alone what we usually do together. Shouldn't I be there, helping out, doing my share?

That these questions are familiar does not make them any less uncomfortable. Bill and I work hard at Meadow Knoll, congenial, companionable work. We share a rich and productive life there, together—the kind of life that any woman in her right mind would envy. (Ah, yes, the practice of Right Mind. A worthy practice.)

And yet, it isn't enough, and that by itself troubles me, for in seeking separation—going somewhere else, doing something else—from my husband and partner, do I trouble him, worry him, injure him? He's never said this, but it's always at the back of my mind. It's my issue rather than his, perhaps, but an issue nevertheless.

These questions bother me. They bothered me the first time I came here, and they bother me now—especially now, perhaps, because we are in the middle of a family crisis, not between us but around us, and this week wasn't the best week to leave. I keep wishing these questions would go away, or that I'd somehow resolve them, but that hasn't happened yet. They're like a plague of gnats buzzing around my ears. Sometimes I can brush them away, sometimes they clamor and bite so urgently that they destroy the very peace I've come to seek. When that happens, I try to remember Rilke's plea "to try to love the questions themselves as if they were locked rooms or books written in a very foreign language. Don't search for the answers, which could not be given to you now, because you would not be able to live them. And the point is to live everything. Live the questions now. Perhaps then, someday far in the future, you will gradually, without even noticing it, live your way into the answer."

So I sit with the questions, and try to let myself love them. Love the questions. Live the questions.

Not an easy answer.

No answer at all. Not yet.

I get up, wash my face, comb my hair, brush away the gnats. Before supper, I'll walk to the Big House and telephone Bill to let him know that I've arrived safely, to make sure that everything is well.

I HAVE A CELL PHONE with me in case of trouble on the road, but the signal fades around Riviera. There's only one telephone line here at Lebh Shomea, a landline, and the phone available to guests is located in a booth in the basement, off the linen room, where the sheets and towels are stored. If the booth is hot, you can turn on a fan and prop the door open. A small sign reminds you to keep your voice down so as not to interrupt the silence of those who may be nearby.

I use my calling card. The phone at Meadow Knoll rings and rings, five times, six times, seven. There's no answer (why doesn't the answering machine pick up?), and I notice a feeling—just a whisper, not a shout—of irritation. Or is it worry? I think it's worry. Bill is always working with power tools, saws and drill presses and the like. He's careful, methodical, and keeps his tools in good condition, but accidents happen. People cut their fingers off with power tools. Cut off their hands, even their arms. Or maybe it's something else, the rain. It was raining when I left, with flooding predicted—maybe the telephone line is down again. To the west of the lake, the creek can flood the road and maroon us until the water goes down. Has there been flooding?

I put down the phone. This is silly. Bill is outside with the dogs, or checking the livestock. It's time for supper; he's gone to Mary's Beef 'N Buns, the local eatery, for a plate of barbeque. But why has he turned off the answering machine?

Momentarily, I wish I knew where he is and what he's doing. Wish I knew that everything is all right and I could stop worrying about him, wish I could tell him that everything here is all right, that I'm loving the silence, that he can stop worrying about me. It's frustrating, not to be able to talk to him.

After a while, I go outside and sit on the step and watch a gray squirrel drinking from a slowly dripping outdoor faucet only a few feet away. Drip drip drip. The squirrel, in no hurry, catches each drop gratefully, as if it were honey, as if it were a prayer. After a while, he sits back on his haunches, rubs his forepaws together, scrubs them over his ears like a cat, and hops gracefully away, a fluid movement, his gray tail rippling like water.

IT MAY ONLY BE a short drive, but I was a long time getting here.

I looked for Lebh Shomea for several years before I found it. I visited several places, but some were too far away, or too busy, or not silent enough. The search was beginning to seem hopeless. And then something odd happened. I woke up from a dream early one morning. The dream was gone but an odd admonition echoed urgently in my mind. *Be alert for messages from me.* Messages? From whom? About what?

I had no idea what this meant, but I recalled it a couple of days later when a woman came up to me after a meditation class I was teaching at the Jung Society in Austin. Without prompting, she said, "I heard about a place you might like," and wrote down the words *Lebh Shomea* on a piece of paper. "It's Catholic," she added, "and pretty far from civilization—no TV, no radio. You can't talk, either. Not a word." She grinned ruefully. "That lets me out. I can't go five minutes without talking."

I tucked the paper into my billfold, along with the credit cards and proof-of-insurance and the kids' phone numbers. A couple of months went by. In Houston to visit Bill's parents, we dropped in on their next-door neighbor, a former Trappist monk. In casual conversation, Bob mentioned Lebh Shomea. I questioned him. Yes, yes, he knew about the place, although he'd never been there. What was the meaning of the name?

"A listening heart," he said.

Ah. A listening heart.

He told me more. Lebh Shomea was a silent Catholic community on a big ranch in South Texas, small, not very well known. Would I like it? I asked. Was it open to non-Catholics? (I had other questions—*Was it open to agnostics? to atheists? to people who sat vipassana instead of praying?*—but I didn't ask them.) He regarded me thoughtfully. "I think it's open, Susan," he said, in his soft way. "And I think—yes, I think you might like it."

Be alert for messages from me. I was listening.

All this occurred before the Internet and Google came along to connect us to everything on the face of the globe. Reaching Lebh Shomea proved difficult. The phone didn't seem to be answered on a regular basis, and it took some digging to locate a mailing address. When I wrote, I received a formal reply from Sister Maria Meister, instructing me to provide a reference who would testify, in writing, to the seriousness of my "interior journey." Serious? Interior journey? It sounded like the place I was looking for.

And so it was, and is. I loved it immediately. Loved the silence above all, loved the surrounding South Texas wilderness, even loved the political intrigue that hangs in the air here, nearly fifty years after Sarita Kenedy East's death in February 1961.

When the Oblates inherited this place, they weren't altogether sure what to do with it. They began by moving St. Peter's Novitiate from La Lomita, Texas, to their new property. But the order established a central novitiate in Illinois, and the last novitiate class left La Parra in 1973. The Oblate Provincial Council pondered, then, in keeping with the global contemplative movement that had grown up after Vatican II, declared it a House of Prayer, giving it the name Lebh Shomea in November 1973. This must have seemed a sensible use for a place in the Wild Horse Desert, which is too remote and inhospitable for all but the most devoted seekers. Not much good, as the community's Web site says, "for anything except encountering God in silence and solitude."

And that is indeed why people come to this place. It fills the deeply felt need for empty space in the midst of our too-busy lives, a place in the "inner psycho-topography of all humans" (as Belden C. Lane has put it), for a desert, a landscape of nothing but sky and land, a wasteland of stark simplicity and sparse comfort that reduces our human pretensions to blown dust and forces us to our knees in the presence of its transcendent mystery.

And so Lebh Shomea became what it is today: a place to encounter God—or whatever name you use for the Sacred—in silence and solitude. It is managed by a core community of three, a priest and two nuns, who are devoted to creating a space for people of all faiths and even of no faith, who feel called to celebrate the spirit within in silence.

Be alert for messages from me.

Yes, listen. It's why I'm here, although after all this time, I'm still not sure what I'm listening for.

CHAPTER ELEVEN

Silence

There is nothing in all the universe so much like God as silence.

MEISTER ECKHART

June 10, 1992. "The more divinity is in things the more divinity is outside of things," Meister Eckhart wrote. Divinity in and through the night, singing through a chorus of coyotes, wild and playful. Divinity this morning, shining through the mysteries of silver fog, lanced with splinters of light.

September 17, 1993. Simple things. Such joy, such richness in the simple, the small, the plain. The light falling across the spotless floor. A birdsong. A bloom on the oleander. Coming here does this for me: it reminds me that less is not just more, less and less and less is all. When I am surrounded by too many things, when my hours are too full of everything, how can I be mindful of any thing?

November 9, 1994. Turkeys still as statues in the early morning light, bronze feathers sun-gilded. Time is still, too, here. No hurry, nothing to do, nowhere in particular to go. Be present where I am, that's all. Be grateful.

IT'S BEEN A QUIET EVENING. Our serve-yourself supper consists of salad, a sandwich of cold cuts and cheese, a handful of raw broccoli and carrots, a bag of chips, a scoop of cottage cheese, a glass of milk. Father Kelly—lithe and wiry, gray-haired, in his sixties—gives me a quick smile and a welcoming nod. But that's the only communication among the nine of us who have gathered for supper.

In silence, we make our salads and sandwiches from food laid out on an oilcloth-covered table, pick up our chips and drinks, and find a place at one of the large round wooden tables in the dining hall. Each is centered with a glass bowl of pink and white oleander blossoms on a rotating wooden tray that holds dining necessities and can be turned so that we don't have to ask our neighbor to pass the salt. People move quietly, respecting the silence, honoring others' solitude. Alone together. Together, alone.

One of Lebh Shomea's practices is called "modesty of the eyes," interpreted as keeping our inquiring or idle glance to ourselves, refraining from intruding upon another's solitude. Acknowledging the other's presence isn't prohibited, of course, but it is often hard to judge whether a glance or a smile is intrusive, so new people tend to keep their eyes, and their smiles, to themselves.

I once held a three-day practicum here, part of a class I was teaching on silence and solitude at the Jung Society. When the group—all women—met back in Austin after our retreat, I asked them to describe the most difficult thing about being silent for three days. Everyone had the same answer. Most of them welcomed the quiet time, the time alone, but mealtimes were a challenge.

This shouldn't have been a surprise, I suppose. Women are taught from childhood that it is our responsibility to maintain the social equilibrium of the group with smiles and gestures, and when this seems discouraged, we're at a loss. One woman said that her face felt "utterly wooden" when she wasn't smiling and talking. Another feared she was "ugly" if her face wasn't decorated with a smile. "I felt terribly unfriendly," said a third. "I was afraid if I didn't speak, people would think I didn't like them, and that made me feel alone and lonely. And unlikable," she added thoughtfully. "If I don't smile, the other person won't smile back. And if she doesn't, it's because she doesn't like me."

Another, a grandmother, said, "All my life, I've done my part at keeping the conversation going. My mother always told me that it was my job to be sure that everybody got some attention. There we were, all together at the dinner table, and I wasn't doing any of the things I've been taught to do. I felt pretty useless." Then she laughed. "I guess that was the point, huh?"

That was the point. One of them, anyway.

I taught this class because (as with so many other subjects) I wanted to learn how I felt about silence, how others experienced it, how they had written about it. The Jung Society generously allowed me to teach it in this exploratory, non-expert, let's-learn-it-together way. So the participants and I read what was available at the time and did our own writing, setting ourselves the task of going apart for a solitary period each week, listening, observing ourselves in the silence, writing down our observations. Witnessing, we called it, borrowing a term from Eastern mystics: allowing our witnessing selves to simply observe without judgment or self-criticism.

Witnessing what we feel, think, do, when we are silent, when we are alone. It's what I do here, now. Listening, observing, witnessing. And writing.

Writing it all down, so I can't forget.

I REACH BILL BY PHONE after supper. The road is muddy but passable, he says, although it's still raining. Two inches in the gauge and another couple of inches predicted overnight, with warnings of severe weather. The lake is already high, and it drains a watershed of fifteen or twenty square miles. This kind of rain means more water coming into the lake. It means flooding on our place. It's worrisome.

Bill went to Mary's for a barbeque plate—our usual evening out together—and the lady behind the counter asked where I was. "She ran away from home," he told her. "No word on whether she'll ever be back." He was joking, he said quickly, just joking.

I hope so, but the gnats are back. I tell Bill this and explain about gnats. He grunts. "I hope they're wearing their water wings," he says.

IT'S TIME FOR BED. I put down my book, set aside the sock I'm knitting for my son, and step outside to look at the stars, astonishingly bright in a very dark sky. Tonight's nearly full moon hasn't risen yet. The air, rain-washed, is sweet with oleander, and the barred owls are out and about with their newly fledged young, the questioning rhythm of the parents' deep eight-note calls (*Who-cooks-for-you? Who-cooks-for-y'all?*) punctuated by the youngsters' raucous hisses and hoots and monkey-like squalls. The young birds are learning from their parents how to hunt the voles, shrews, and deer mice they live on. Owls down their prey whole, digest it, and regurgitate the indigestible scraps of bone and fur in the form of neat, dry pellets. Last year, walking along one of the several nature trails that wander through the thorny brush, I found a heap of owl pellets under a mesquite tree and looked up to see a talon-scarred branch, an owl's favorite perch. There's something wonderful about a place that's home to owls.

There are no security lights here, and the land is so flat that any light pollution from Corpus Christi, seventy miles to the north, isn't visible above the horizon. Punctuating the dark, I see the flickering gleams of fireflies, bright as falling stars. We have only a few at Meadow Knoll, but here there are many. They're active until almost midnight on dark nights and seem to switch themselves off when the moon is very bright. Both the male and the female turn on, I've read, although the males are brighter. Each species has its own special code, flickering on and off at specific intervals, the secret, silent come-hither of firefly courtship. But the signals can be dangerous, for some fireflies have cannibalistic appetites. They light their lamps as a decoy: "Hey, beautiful, I'm over here. Come have a little bite of something with me." *Be alert for messages from me* (but do be alert).

Visible among the firefly sparks and sparkles are the stationary glimmers of lights behind the blinds in a few of the dwellings and in the library at the Big House. There are no other signs of life, no sounds except for the owls' calls. I close the door and go inside, into my private space, so neat and orderly. My books are on the shelves, I've turned the plastic book crate into a footstool, and my jeans and shirts are hung in the closet. Simple, satisfying household arrangements, all I need.

And I've managed to set aside my worries about what's going on at home, at least for the moment. Maybe the rain will stop. Maybe there won't be serious flooding. Bill is perfectly capable of handling any emergencies over the week I plan to be here. I'll miss him, yes, but not just yet, not very much. Being here, being solitary, being silent—it's all too new, too fresh, too sweet.

THE NEW DAY BEGINS with the slow, mindful ringing of the Angelus bell, which goes back to eleventh-century monastic custom. Three tolls and a pause, three tolls and a pause, three tolls and a pause, then nine tolls. The ringing is a devotion, taking its name from the words, *Angelus Domini nuntiavit Mariae* (the angel of the Lord declared to Mary). In the monasteries, the Angelus was rung at 6 a.m., noon, and 6 p.m. At Lebh Shomea, it is rung a half-hour before Mass, just before dinner, and just before supper. It speaks: waken, listen, prepare. And I hear: mystery, blessing, grace, Word incarnate.

Be alert for messages from me.

The bell itself, which hangs near the west entrance to the Big House, is said to have come from one of Captain Mifflin Kenedy's side-wheelers, designed especially to navigate the shallow waters of the Rio Grande during the Civil War—boats that carried cotton in one direction and Confederate guns in the other. Now, instead of raising an alarm or announcing an arrival, it summons to contemplation and to the day's regular duties: a nice irony, it seems to me.

I rise, dress, and make my bed. The sun will be up in a few moments, and I look out the window to see wisps of silver fog trailing through shadowy trees. I wonder whether it rained at Meadow Knoll overnight, and if so, how much, and whether there's flooding. It's cool here, and a sweatshirt will be a good idea. I hurry into jeans and a shirt, splash my face with water, and tidy my hair, at the cheerful urging of a mockingbird practicing his dawn song in a nearby mesquite tree. This bird is a whole choir of bird singers, all singing at once. And he doesn't confine himself to birdsongs, like other single-minded choristers. He's celebrating frogs and crickets, cats and dogs, a bobwhite calling, water splashing, a gate swinging, children laughing. *Mimus polyglottos*, a mimic of many tongues. The Rule of Silence was not explained to him, and I am glad.

The day begins with the celebration of the Eucharist in the Chapel of the Little Children, to which I walk in the company of ghostly figures wrapped in fog and silence. Inside, I leave my shoes and take one of the straight chairs aligned in a precise semicircle before the cloth-covered altar table and the lectern on which the Scriptures rest, beneath a large cross of rough-hewn planks hung against the plain terra-cotta wall. The number of chairs depends upon the number of guests, and a vacant chair suggests that someone has slept through the Angelus. "At the time of the rising dawn," St. John of the Cross wrote in *Spiritual Canticle*, "silent music, sounding solitude, the supper that refreshes, and deepens love."

Father Kelly celebrates Mass in a white alb and stole, worn over his daily working garb of khakis and tee shirt. He opens the service with a glance that acknowledges each person, a clear, direct greeting to each of us individually. "The Lord is with each one of you," he says, and even I, poised on the razor of my everlasting doubt, feel embraced by the comfort of the words. Here is the Lord, here in me, in the others, in each, in all. Hear. Listen.

The ritual is simple and always the same: an introductory prayer, a reading from Scripture, followed by the Offertory, the Eucharist Prayer, and Communion. There is a brief person-to-person sharing of reflections on a word in the Scripture reading that catches our attention. The Gospel reading for this day is from John 8:12–20 and includes the words of Jesus: "Even if I bear witness of myself, my witness is true." The word—the Word—that calls out to me: *witness*.

Yes, witness. It is what I am here for, to bear witness of myself, to Self, true witness, the truest I can manage. That's what this writing is about. I hope it's true.

When I first began coming to Lebh Shomea, I was not comfortable at Mass. As a child, I went to my mother's evangelical church, which read the Bible literally, measured all moral issues in black and white, and viewed the Roman Catholic Church (as well as Mormonism, Buddhism, Hinduism, and Judaism) as devilishly misguided. Having rejected those teachings, having moved through the atheism of my youth and into an inclusive agnosticism of middle age, I felt alienated from the ritual of Communion. Some large part of me felt like a phony, coming to Lebh Shomea for the richness of silence and solitude but not believing, at least, not in the way the people of this community believe. I had rejected belief. What I had were questions.

But Father Kelly, a wise and practical man, reminded me that faith is deeper and stronger than belief. "God is larger than you think," he said. "Larger than we know." Faith—faith in the Utmost, the Inexpressible, the All-There-Is—*that* is the mystery, and it is in search of this faith that I am here. Not to know, not to believe, not even to look for answers. But to have faith that the questions matter. To live the questions without hoping that the answers will come.

That is what I remember during this morning's Communion, as I envy the others' secure belief and share, as far as I am able, their generous, their unfathomed faith. As the mesquite tree outside the window shimmers with the gold of the rising sun. As a cardinal, vivid as a splash of heart's blood, cries out in the silence, *What cheer! What cheer! What cheer!*

CHAPTER TWELVE

Seeing Through Time

All inhabited landscapes carry markers if we can learn their vocabulary—sculpted mounds, piles of stones, divided fields, a circle of ash, a single tree left in an open pasture to grow old. . . . We need reading lessons.

DEBORAH TALL, *FROM WHERE WE STAND:*
RECOVERING A SENSE OF PLACE

To be human is to live in a world that is filled with significant places: to be human is to have and to know your place.

E. RELPH, *PLACE AND PLACELESSNESS*

February 23, 1996. There is a restful sense of timelessness here at Lebh Shomea. Every day is so much like every other day in sweet, mysterious succession. But looking deeper, under the surface, you can see the marks of previous occupations, earlier uses, earlier peoples, another order. It would be lovely to think of nature without man, but that's not possible here or anywhere the land is marked by human-caused change. Coming to know a place means coming to know its human past—the land explored, invaded, inhabited—not just its present.

December 21, 1997. I often think of the prehistoric cultures that moved through this silent place—grasslands, then, along this coastal bend, an infinite, endless savanna of grass—finding enough to sustain them, depending on the fruits of the land, of the lagoon inside the barrier islands, of the river bottoms. I think of the way they must have understood this place, not as a wilderness but as a known and loved refuge, a rich and abundant homeland. And how they must have understood time, too, not as something passing, here and gone, but as return and repetition: the sun's travel across the daily sky, the endless cycles of seasons, their own movement through space, which was time. In this sense, the timelessness of Lebh Shomea, measured in the daily rituals and repetitions, is closer to the way the earliest human inhabitants experienced this place.

I LEAVE THE CHAPEL and head back to the Big House for breakfast, taking in deep breaths of the clean, crisp air, flavored with . . . what?

It is the unmistakable musky perfume of collared peccary, a half dozen of them. We occasionally see these barrel-shaped, gray-brown javelinas at Meadow Knoll, and when we do, they are wild and unapproachable. But although these creatures are fierce-looking—*javelina* comes from the Spanish word for sword—they have as little concern about my presence as the deer that graze outside my window. A black, coarse-bristled sow and her four young are foraging ravenously under the oaks for undiscovered acorns, snorting, sniffling, scuffling, chuckling over their finds, a soft chorus of delight. Mesquite beans, *lechuguilla* (a species of agave), and the plentiful prickly pear cactus—these are on their breakfast menu as well, especially the pads and (in season) ripe red tunas of the prickly pear, which have a high water content. How these animals manage to eat this forbidding cactus is a mystery. Henri Joutel, one of the few who survived La Salle's ill-fated 1685 landing at Matagorda Bay, remarked on the danger of eating the "fig," as he called the prickly pear fruit: "One must strip the fruit before eating it because, although the quills are quite small and almost imperceptible, without fail they make one sick once they lodge in the throat and on the roof of the mouth. One of our soldiers even died from having eaten the fig greedily without wiping it. All these quills caused tremendous inflammation of the throat and eventually suffocated him."

My breakfast is easier and more pleasant. In the dining room at the Big House, I fill a bowl with cereal, add raisins and a sliced banana, and find milk and juice in the refrigerator. I toast a slice of bread in the toaster on a shelf in the corner and take a place at a table where I can look out the window and see a palm tree framed against the morning sky.

The dining room, like the other spaces here, is immaculate and tidy, glasses arranged in crystal rows on one open shelf and mugs on another, above the coffee pots and hot water for tea. When we've eaten, we take our dishes and tableware to a pass-through window into the kitchen, where we put them into the appropriate bins: china and glassware, silver, paper, composting scraps. The kitchen is designed to feed a crowd, with large ranges and a walk-in cooler where fresh beef is hung. The cooking and kitchen chores are done by staff and guests. Those who stay for more than ten days are asked to do an hour's manual labor a day in the kitchen, garden, or office. Those who stay more than twenty days put in two hours of daily work. Most of us here are short-termers and pay a modest stipend for our bed and board. I am selfishly glad to be spared both the cooking and the dishes, chores that Bill and I share at home.

At the thought of Bill, I decide to call and see what the weather is like. The phone rings until the answering machine picks up.

"Just checking to see if you've been washed away yet," I say cheerily. But I wish I knew what was going on there. Solitude and silence are wonderful, but sometimes you need to be in touch.

I'VE BEEN LOOKING FORWARD with pleasure to visiting the library again. It occupies the main floor of this large house, rooms that once served as the Kenedy family's drawing room, dining room, library, and study. It's a somber space, gloomy, some might say, and still retains hints of old opulence, the walls mahogany-paneled, the ceilings beamed, the windows arched, some of stained glass. When Sarita, her husband, and her parents moved into the newly built house in 1923, there were crystal chandeliers, Oriental rugs, Louis XIV furniture, oil paintings, and sculpture, even a death mask of Napoleon Bonaparte. I've never seen it, but I've read that Don Gregorio installed a walk-in safe in his office, with a trapdoor that opened into a basement tunnel and a fortified bunker a hundred yards away—not a surprising precaution, given the periodic violence that threatened this area for a great many years.

But for all its richness, *La Casa Grande* does not seem to have been a happy home. By the time the house was completed, Sarita's mother and father knew that the third generation of Kenedys would be the last. Sarita had fallen ill with undulant fever in the early years of her marriage to Arthur East and could not bear children. Sarita's older brother Johnny (who engaged in periodic bouts with the bottle) had caught mumps in 1913, not long after his marriage to Elena Seuss, and was sterile as well—at least, that's the family's story.

(Which may or may not be true. A Corpus Christi man, Ray Fernandez, claims that his mother Ann, born in 1925 to an unmarried La Parra housemaid named Maria Rowland, is Johnny Kenedy's daughter and entitled to a share of the Kenedy estate. Preliminary DNA results seem to suggest a relationship, and a judge ordered that Johnny's body be exhumed for more detailed analysis. The case is stalled in the Texas courts. Nobody would be surprised if it dragged on for decades.)

The luxurious Kenedy furnishings are gone now, and books take their place. The collection is substantial: some thirty thousand volumes by hundreds of authors, many in original languages. There's a card catalog, idiosyncratic but easy to use, once you understand it; a media room with audio and videotapes; a good-sized Texana collection; and reference books on the area's natural history. The library is air-conditioned, not for the comfort of its users but for the welfare of the books in this hot, humid climate. Still, on sweltering July and August days, this is as cool, and as dry, as it gets.

Libraries (like bookstores) hold a special transformative magic for me. When I was a child, Danville's small Carnegie Library was only a block from my paternal grandmother's apartment. I'd spend whole Saturdays reading in the silence, until I was fetched home with as many books as I could carry in two shopping bags. I even fantasized that if the bomb were dropped nearby (this was in the early 1950s and the bomb was on everyone's mind), I would hide in the library. If I had to die, I would die reading. Years later, I wept at the bitter irony of a *Twilight Zone* episode called "Time Enough at Last." Spectacled, bookish Henry Bemis, a dull little man whose greatest, whose only passion is reading, runs to the library when the bomb destroys his town. Ah, books and the leisure with which to read them—until he breaks his glasses.

I understood Henry Bemis. I ached for Henry Bemis. In some ways, I suppose, I am Henry Bemis. When I go into a library, I feel as if I am being embraced by books and by the spirits of their authors, a swelling, polyphonic chorus, speaking to me in silence. I feel awe and an enormous sense of privilege: how many people across how many centuries of civilization have had access to such riches of knowledge? And as I walk down the row of shelves, picking up this book, that book, another, the awe is always mixed with anticipation. Who knows what new authors I'll stumble across, what new fascinations will tempt me? I might discover something that will change my life. It's happened before. It can happen again, any day now, Henry Bemis. I carry a spare set of glasses, just in case.

Something on the wall, over a bookshelf, catches my eye. It's a framed aerial photograph of the area surrounding the Big House when it was still the La Parra Ranch headquarters, sometime in the 1940s. Perhaps it was taken when Johnny died in 1948, when the ranch was divided between Sarita and her sister-in-law Elena, Johnny's widow. The dwellings and the new chapel don't appear in the photo; they were constructed after the Missionary Oblates came.

But there in the center is the massive *Casa Grande*, fronted on the east by the formal palm-lined avenue and the expanse of mown lawn. At the rear are the buildings that belonged to the working ranch: barns, bunkhouses, a blacksmith shop, an icehouse, a garage, and a water-powered turbine that generated electricity. Out of the picture is the Cowboy Cemetery, where the Kenedy vaqueros and their families are buried, but in the picture is the Kenedy family cemetery with its large Lourdes grotto, constructed of Texas limestone. (That's where Johnny Kenedy's body awaits the wisdom of the courts.) Beside it is the Sacred Heart Chapel, where Father Kelly celebrates Mass on Sundays and holidays for local ranch families and Lebh Shomea's guests.

It's an arresting photograph. Studying it, I find myself looking for signs of this present in that past, the *now* in that *then*. Here, in the future, in my own new millennium, stands the Chapel of the Little Children, where I attended Mass this morning. There is Ezekiel, where I slept last night; there Jeremiah, where I stayed last year and the year before that. And Sophia, where I woke one night to the calling of an owl just outside my window. The photograph, a time fixed in space, a space fixed in time, bridges La Parra Ranch and the House of Prayer, defines the territory of each, of both, as a pattern of relationships and responsibilities, of care for land and people, each in a different way. *We need reading lessons*, as Deborah Tall reminds us. Yes.

One of the things that stands out in this photograph is the open land, grazing land, that surrounded La Parra's ranch headquarters. In those days, some sixty years ago, Sarita managed it as a working ranch, from all reports a model of good grazing pastures, stocked with her favorite Santa Gertrudis cattle. Things have changed. Driving up the ranch road yesterday, I didn't see acres of open savanna where cattle could graze. I saw thickets of thorny brush and low trees, mesquite, retama, huisache.

I find myself wishing for a current aerial photo of this place. There isn't one, at least not here, but there's something better. I'll climb up to the lookout tower on top of the house. I stash my books in a corner, check the log at the bottom of the landing to be sure that the tower room is not already occupied by someone seeking solitude, and head for the stairs. Up three flights, four. The stairs become steeper with each flight until they are almost a ladder.

Sarita climbed up here, too, in the years after her husband died, a glass of Scotch in her hand, or maybe a bottle. When she was a little drunk, the servants said, she would sing the country and western songs she danced to in earlier days. What did she see when she looked out across the savanna? How did she feel, knowing that there would be no heirs of Kenedy blood—on the right side of the matrimonial divide, anyway—to carry on the work of the ranch? Did she think about the days when she was an energetic young girl, a tomboy, a vaquera who was happiest on a horse, riding with her vaqueros to work the cows? Did she think about change, about the way the land would change when she was no longer here to be its steward? Did she try to plan ways to keep this land just as it was?

Breathing hard, I arrive at the top, the lookout tower, and gaze out over the land. I'm mesmerized. In one sense, there's nothing to be seen, nothing but flat earth and sky and sun, burning sun, and flickering shadows of clouds. Nothing, nothing at all but hundreds of thousands of acres of solitude, silence. It's a vastly vacant landscape, deserted, empty. Boring, too, I suppose, if you're looking for dramatic heights, breathtaking depths, spectacular seas, or architectural wonders.

I'm looking for grass. I'm gazing across a flat sea of mesquite, enameled green under a sapphire sky brushed with wisps of white cloud, gilded by morning sun. To the east lies a gleaming silver blade, Baffin Bay, and evidence of brush-clearing projects designed to restore some of the native grasses that grew on this plain since the ancient seas receded into the Gulf. The grass was never very plentiful here, measured as pasturage for confined cattle. I've read estimates of anywhere between fifteen and forty-five acres for a cow-calf pair. On the Illinois prairies of my childhood, where the grass is definitely greener, it takes only two acres to support a cow-calf pair. To feed a lot of cows here, you'd need a lot of acres, a lot of good grass. The rancher would have to husband the grass, look after it, protect it.

But as I look to the west and south, I see little visible grass, except for the neatly-clipped emerald lawns that surround the Big House. As far as I can see, there is nothing but brush—scrubby mesquite, spindly oak, wild persimmon, huisache, ebony, brazil bush. This was what Sarita was fighting off, keeping at bay.

It wasn't like this when the Europeans arrived some four centuries ago. Then it was open savanna, coastal grasslands with only isolated clumps of trees and bushes, burned to the roots in the frequent fires that raced through the dry plains. The French, coming to harvest souls, brought only their Bibles. But the Spanish brought their cows and horses, and the animals, unfenced, unchecked, abandoned, ran wild. They feasted with relish on the sugary pods of mesquite and on acorns and persimmons and the fruits of other shrubs, leaving behind an expansive, well-fertilized wake of not-quite-digested seeds that sprouted and grew into impenetrable clumps of brush. Flourishing, the herds grew to enormous size, their progeny as perfectly adapted to the land as any wild species, as any deer or buffalo or javelina here on *Los Llanos Mesteños*.

Mesteños? The *Novísimo Diccionario* of 1888 defines the word: "Wild, having no master. Said of both horses and cattle." The longhorn cow, the mustang horse, *mesteños* both.

Los Llanos Mesteños. The Desert of the Wild Ones.

A fine place for hermits.

CHANGE IS IN THE nature of things, change across a sea of time, across time unimaginable, time out of mind.

I know from my reading in the library downstairs that the earliest human inhabitants of this area belonged to a culture that archaeologists call the Aransas group. Nobody quite knows where the Aransans came from. When they arrived, the Gulf that I can glimpse out there lay miles farther to the east, the shoreline advancing and receding as glacial ice ages advanced and retreated and sea levels rose and fell. Shell tools excavated at various sites tell us that these peoples camped along this shore around 7,500 B.P. ("before the present," as archaeologists say, with the "present" being 1950, when radiocarbon dating began to be used). The Aransans harvested oysters and shellfish for a living until rising sea levels pushed them inland, but they were back again by 6,000 B.P., with a new technology: chipped flint spear points.

Around three thousand years ago, the Gulf stabilized at more or less its current level, the barrier islands formed, and the enclosed and protected lagoons and bays sheltered a wide variety of plants, fish, and shellfish. A thousand years ago, early Native Americans (descendents of the Aransans or immigrants from some other area) began to exploit the rich resources of sea and land. Nomads, they moved seasonally from camp to camp along the shore, often in dugout canoes, fishing and harvesting shellfish from fall through early spring. In the summer, they trekked inland to camps in the river valleys, where they hunted white-tailed deer, bison, turkey, and javelina and gathered the abundant wild grapes—mustang grapes, *mesteños*. In late summer, they moved to areas where there were large stands of prickly pear, to harvest the fruit. In autumn, they went back to the river valleys for pecans and acorns. Over time, their technologies became more complex: they adopted bows and arrows for hunting and began making baskets as containers for storage.

I look out across the green forest, imagining these hunter-gatherers camped along Baffin Bay, to the east, just over there. They were a close-knit community, relying on each other in what must have been a powerful relationship between persons and place in the midst of this vast, silent emptiness. I imagine them camping beside their ancestors' middens, fishing with spears or catching fish in weirs constructed of cane or with bone hooks and lines made from the twisted ligaments of agave, smoking the fish, salting it. I see the women taking down the huts and folding the hide coverings and loading them into the canoes, traveling to another site to harvest the ripe prickly pear fruit, which they might steam or roast in oven-pits or dry and press flat. I think of them fashioning the large green prickly pear pads into canteens to carry water or using the pounded flesh as poultices to treat wounds and ulcers, or to brew a medicinal tea

And I think of the profound intimacy with which these people must have known their country, the maps they must have held in their minds, the remembered, retold stories that guided them to a bed of fine oysters or a place where many redfish and drum might be caught, or to a pecan grove on an inland river, or to a plentiful harvest of mesquite beans or acorns or prickly pear fruit. Like other aboriginal peoples, they would have depended on a rich, long-held, and ever-expanding store of place-memory, would have participated in the communal clan-consciousness of significant locations and the trails that led to them. We have no record of their spiritual practice, but the world they lived in must have been entirely sacred, landmarked by places that were a refuge and an inspiration and watched over by place-spirits whose protection and guidance they continually sought.

This early culture was followed in the historic period by a people who came to be collectively called the Karankawa. They were tall (some say seven feet), well-built, and imposing, decorated with fierce-looking tattoos, paint, and piercings. They pursued much the same way of life as their predecessors, living in large fishing camps on the shore in the winter, separating into smaller parties for hunting and plant-gathering in the other seasons, and coming together again for fishing. Their red cedar bows were as long as they were tall, and they are reported to have had great strength as archers, capable of firing arrows with extraordinary accuracy at distances of more than two hundred yards. Inaccurately depicted by the Spanish as primitive scavengers who lived a hand-to-mouth existence in an unfriendly land, they were instead highly skilled and deeply resourceful in their use of all that this land of estuary and savanna and river bottom offered to them. The success of these people, W. W. Newcomb says,

> was compounded of a willingness to utilize virtually everything in their environment . . . which in turn depended on an intimate knowledge of their land—what each plant was good for, when fruits in certain places would be ripe, where elusive game could be taken.

The Karankawa met their first white man in 1528. He was Cabeza de Vaca, and he and his shipmates were shipwrecked near Galveston on what he called (with some justification) "The Island of Ill Fate." De Vaca was one of eighty survivors of a three hundred-member expedition that had set out to conquer and colonize the area around the Gulf from Florida to eastern Mexico, already claimed for Spain. Only a few, including de Vaca, lived to tell the tale.

And what a tale it was. The Karankawa, who proved friendly and accommodating, gathered up the men, treated their injuries, and gave them food and shelter. The enterprising de Vaca learned what he could from them and then moved on, becoming a trader and sometime medicine man and acquainting himself with the ways of the native peoples he encountered. He and three others eventually made their way across what is now South Texas and Mexico to Culiacán, an outpost near the Pacific coast, where they arrived—to the great astonishment of all—in early 1536. De Vaca did exactly what many of us would have done under the circumstances: he wrote a book about his journey into the interior, to which we owe most of our knowledge of these peoples' way of life.

It was through their next encounter with Europeans that the Karankawas got their unfortunate reputation for savagery. In 1685, nearly one hundred and sixty years after de Vaca, a group of French expeditionaries under René Robert Cavalier, Sieur de La Salle, trying to locate the Mississippi River, blundered into Karankawa country. They built Fort St. Louis on Lavaca Bay and claimed the area for France (in spite of the fact that the Spanish were already calling it New Spain).

Unfortunately, La Salle got his enterprise off on the wrong foot by appropriating several of the Karankawas' dugout canoes, which might have been loaned to him, if he'd taken the trouble to ask. Not long after, smallpox broke out and the Europeans began to die. Things went from bad to worse, and in March 1686 La Salle was assassinated by his followers, who (understandably) blamed him for getting them into this mess. The Karankawas raided the little fort, killed the survivors, and made off with five children, who were adopted into the tribe. France's short tenure had ended, and Spain went on with its conquests.

Almost a century after La Salle, Fray Gaspar José de Solis, a priest sent to inspect Spanish missions, accused the Karankawas of cannibalism—specifically of cutting celebratory pieces from a living prize of war and roasting them over the fire. "They do the same thing with the priests and Spaniards if they catch any," de Solis added in hushed horror.

In spite of the fact that de Solis had not witnessed this appalling event himself but only heard about it, and regardless of de Vaca's testimony that the

Karankawas were appalled when the Spanish ate their own dead to stay alive, the charge of cannibalism stuck, along with other disagreeable attributes. Until I came to Lebh Shomea and began learning something about the real lives of the people who had occupied this land in the past, the only thing I knew about the Karankawas was the distasteful fact that they ate their victims, as well as harvesting undigested seeds from their feces and eating them again. Oh, and they smelled. "There arises from their bodies such a stench that it causes one who is little accustomed to them to become sick at the stomach," reported one fastidious father.

Obviously not the kind of people you'd invite to dinner—at least, that was how they were described by those who wanted to be rid of them, or who would like them to wash. But the Spanish kept trying. They established several missions in the area and invited the Karankawas to accept their hospitality and the religion that went with the offer. The Karankawas, however, stubbornly preferred their nomadic walkabouts to the domesticity of mission life. But under threat by the Comanches and Apaches who were pushing in from the west, a few found refuge and were converted at the Spanish mission at Refugio.

Still, most Karankawas clung to the land that had fed their bodies and spirits for something like half a millennium. They were never as fiercely defiant as were the Plains Indians, but they were certainly not as compliant as the Tonkawas. They resisted the blandishments of the priests, preferring not to be Christianized, missionized, or washed. They ignored the settlers moving into their territory and persisted in following the familiar trails across the ancient land to their long-held fishing and hunting and gathering grounds.

This uncomfortable state of affairs continued until 1821, when the newly independent Mexican government began to offer land grants to encourage increased settlement in what was now called Tejas. The new ranchers and farmers, Norteños, became annoyed at the Karankawas' habit of trespassing, willy-nilly, on their newly acquired land. The Karankawas, for their part, doggedly went on doing exactly as they had been doing for as long as they could remember, trekking from their ancestors' oyster beds to the pecan groves to the prickly pear plantations and back again. Relations between the settlers and the nomads became increasingly uncomfortable, and finally Stephen F. Austin (known as the "Father of Texas") declared that the only solution was extermination. (When I think of this, the phrase from Joseph Conrad's *Heart of Darkness* echoes sadly in my mind: "Exterminate the brutes.")

This took a while. Austin and a group of settlers clashed with the Karankawas, resulting in casualties and hard feelings on both sides. A treaty was arranged, then another, honored by neither settlers nor Indians, and the skirmishing dragged on. But time was not on the Indians' side, and within twenty years, all of Karankawa country was fenced by farmers and pastured by ranchers. The Karankawas themselves were either killed by disease or forced farther and farther south until they ended up on the other side of the Rio Grande. But their hearts were always in the land to which they belonged, and when a small band attempted to return to the home of their ancestors, they were annihilated. This invisible, voiceless people had gone into silent oblivion.

The great Texas naturalist, Roy Bedichek, spent much of his life wandering the tidelands and wild places of the Texas coast that once were the sacred places of the Karankawas. He nourished a long-held admiration for this doomed tribe, perhaps because he himself was a renegade, standing staunchly against the philosophy of "nature in service of man" that dominated his era and fiercely respectful of those who lived lightly and thriftily upon the resources of the natural world. "The Karánkaways are gone," he wrote with a sad irony, when he himself was past seventy. "Only bitter memories of them remain. In the minds of our people they are eternally damned, largely because they refused a culture we offered, resisting our proffered blessings to the last."

The people who preferred the desert, *Los Llanos Mesteños*, the Desert of the Wild Ones, had disappeared.

CHAPTER THIRTEEN

Spirits of the Place
El Desierto de los Muertos

I sit in the cool back room, where words cease to resound, where
all meanings are absorbed in the *consonantia* of heat, fragrant pine,
quiet wind, bird song and one central tonic note that is unheard and
unmuttered. This is no longer a time of obligations.

THOMAS MERTON, *THE TRUE SOLITUDE*

And places themselves are the present expressions of past experiences
and events and of hopes for the future.

E. RELPH, *PLACE AND PLACELESSNESS*

September 10, 1998. When I wake here in the middle of the night, I lie very still, breathing like a tree, bending to the breath of . . . God.

May 14, 2000. Walked down the sandy trail past the Community Center to the Cowboy Cemetery this morning. Such silence, such an expanse of spirit, of light. Life's work done, workers laid to rest, human effort finished. What's left?

October 23, 2003. I'm thinking of the work Bill and I have done at Meadow Knoll, and trying to imagine how much work went into this place, when it was a ranch. Trying to imagine the effort, the dogged determination, the sheer strength of will and resolute commitment it took to force this land to produce what men wanted it to produce. Cows, mostly, when there was enough rain to keep the grass going. Or cotton—but the cotton failed. Oil, finally, most profitably, although that will be gone, too, eventually.

But here at Lebh Shomea, what counts is soul-time. That's all that matters, in the end. That's all there is.

BACK FROM THE LIBRARY, I take off my shoes and open Ezekiel's windows (guests are cautioned to close doors and windows when they leave, even for a few moments, because of sudden showers). I pull out my meditation bench and sit for a while, getting quiet, getting still, remembering the reasons I'm here. Feeling more settled, I spend the rest of the morning reading Thomas Merton. He loved silence, coveted solitude, begged to be allowed to leave his Trappist community for a hermitage. Merton would be at home here in *Los Llanos Mesteños*. He would covet Ezekiel, the solitude, the silence—well, perhaps not covet, since he prayed to move beyond desire. But it would have felt right to him.

Still, I'm restless. Maybe it's the invisible spirits of the Karankawas in their dugout canoes, poling through the shallow waters inside the barrier reef islands, blown by winds of change they cannot control, to which they cannot even respond, silently, inexorably flickering into extinction like a candle in a hurricane. Maybe it's the knowledge that the Karankawas are only one of the tribes of Texas Indians hounded out of their homelands so that their places could be appropriated by newcomers fired and inspired by other gods, other goods. That they are only one of the thousands of Indian bands—Cherokee, Choctaw, Apache, Comanche—who suffered this same fate across the country we call ours. That the only way we could have our places was to take them from those who were already in place there.

And what becomes of deeply rooted people whose places are taken? When they lose their place, do they lose their identity? That is what happened to the Karankawas, who left no trace of their centuries on the land, no fragment of language, no settlements, only a few artifacts of shell, bone, flint. Displaced people, they have vanished from the face of the earth, gone forever, leaving only a ghostly presence behind.

Compared to these rooted peoples, our modern culture is rootless, placeless. We love our homes, but for many of us they are financial investments, status symbols. How far and how often we are able to trade up—to a larger, more elegant house, to better schools, to a more exclusive neighborhood—is an outward and visible sign of our success in the career culture.

But even we privileged Americans can see what happens to people who have lost their place. Look at the victims of 2005 Hurricanes Katrina and Rita, who can never return to the homes, to the neighborhoods, to the city they loved. At farmers who have lost their family farms. At homeless people who have suffered a complete disconnect from society. If even our placeless culture can feel the desperate, despairing pain of loss of place, isn't it likely that native peoples, more deeply, more intimately connected to the land than we, felt an even more excruciating pain, like that of an amputation?

Uneasily, I put Merton aside and go to the window, resting my forehead against the cool pane. Two rabbits sit motionless in the grass, their ears so translucent that I can see the pink veins pulsing blood. A spotted fawn is curled up under an oleander, the doe grazing nearby. A green jay flashes through the trees, a large, exotic bird with a violet-blue patch on his head, black mask and bib, and bright yellow feathers on both sides of his tail. He—or perhaps this is a she, for both wear the same gaudy tropical outfit year-round—is native to this southern tip of Texas, to the savannas and thorny brush. This is his habitat, his place; his boisterous, raucous rattle can be heard nowhere else in the United States.

But unlike the invisible, voiceless Karankawa, the green jay would be missed and mourned if he disappeared. His absence would be remarked, the reasons discussed, debated. Visiting birders (tourists make an important contribution to the economy of this region) would have one fewer remarkable bird to add to their life-lists.

I sigh. Maybe it's just the weather, this unsettled feeling. The day is heating up, becoming more sultry, more humid. The dry palm fronds hang motionless, soundless. There's not a whisper of breeze. A storm is rising miles to the east over the Gulf, thunderheads billowing like fabulous pillows, white and blue against a still-blue sky. We'll have rain this afternoon. I frown. Is it raining at home? Flooding? Is everything all right?

I could go to the phone booth and try to call, but not getting through would be frustrating. I should try to disconnect myself. After all, I'm here on retreat, here to be alone. I'm supposed to be in the present, in the now, in the solitary *here*. If my thoughts are always there, what's the use?

I'm ready to stretch my legs, ready for fresh air, for a walk. I fill a canteen, stuff my poncho into my fanny pack, and take my camera. As I step out onto the path, I see Father Kelly on the golf cart he uses to get around. He's wearing a white cowboy hat and a long-sleeved shirt against the sun. We exchange a wave, and I set off.

I AM AIMING TO GO NOWHERE, which is an unusual kind of walking for me. In an ordinary, purpose-driven life, there is no time to waste, no energy to spend on unproductive activities. But what do I have to do here with time, or time with me? I'm not wearing a watch. The only thing I have to do, *want* to do, is listen. Listen and witness. It's enough.

Lebh Shomea's thousand acres are webbed with nature trails. I take the lane between the garage and the Community Center and set off southeastward. This path is a two-lane sandy track, which makes for easy walking through the thorny brush—easy enough that I can practice walking meditation: simply walking, with attention to each movement, attention to each breath. No thought, just watching, witnessing, beholding. Yes, that's the word. I think of something Diane Ackerman wrote in *The Moon by Whale Light*: "There is a way of beholding nature that is itself a form of prayer."

Walking like this is walking inside a prayer, walking slowly and then slower, focusing on being, not going, not needing to be anywhere in particular. Seeing with soft eyes, unfocused, taking in a wide view. Hearing with soft ears. I remember a *gatha* someone once taught me, a short prayer said in Buddhist practice, and say it aloud as I walk, walking with awareness, paying attention to my breath, taking a couple of steps for each in-breath and each out-breath.

> Breathing in, I am arriving;
> > breathing out, I am home.
> Breathing in, I am here;
> > breathing out, this is now.
> Breathing in, I am rooted;
> > breathing out, I am free.
> Breathing in, I dwell;
> breathing out, in the ultimate.

In this way, I go along, just walking, not hurrying, silently repeating the *gatha*, listening to my breathing. Hearing the crisp *pit-a-see, pit-a-see* of a vermilion flycatcher, scarlet-bellied with a scarlet cap. The *peter peter peter* of a black-crested tufted titmouse. The brilliant whistles of an Altamira oriole, feathers bright as new gold, bill like polished ebony.

Ah, yes, the oriole. Someone has collected several oriole nests and hung them on the door to the library. Wondrously constructed, they are like long stockings, artfully woven of the inner bark of trees, of Spanish moss, retama leaves, dried grasses. I stop to admire the intricate industry each time I enter the library.

Oriole nests. I'm distracted, I'm thinking, but no matter. *Breathing in, I have arrived.* I take several more steps, pulling my attention to the breath, feeling the shift of the sand underfoot, shifting my balance on the uneven ground. I hear a fierce, clacking chatter and turn. My eye catches a glimpse of violent orange. I peer through the green lace curtain of a retama tree, embroidered with sweet golden blossoms, and blink. I can see nothing but the brilliant, blinding fire of orioles, five, ten, a dozen, orange flags fluttering furiously. Is it a snake they're after? A green snake, perhaps, curling like innocent smoke along a thorny green branch, intent on raiding an oriole's nest?

No, not a snake. It's an owl, a small owl hunkered down on a branch, silent as a statue, impervious to the orioles' fierce clatter. He's pretending he's not there, or that they're not there, or something. His golden beak is polished, golden eyes round and unblinking against the orange lightning of the orioles, feathers fluffed, ruffed around his shoulders like a cape to ward off the shower of orange sparks. The orioles are warning him away from a nest, from eggs, from young. The scene is as violent as a storm, as exotic as a tropical jungle, as perfect as a poem.

There's a feather on the ground, brilliant orange, an oriole feather. I pick it up and hold it. It feels like a sign, a gift.

Be alert for messages from me.

Word from the orioles, silence from the owl, in the Wild Horse Desert.

WALKING AGAIN.
Breathing in, I am rooted; breathing out, I am free.
Walking, in this place, in place.
Walking with orioles.
Walking with owls.

BREATHING OUT, THIS IS NOW.
I do not admire theme parks, with their inauthentic, kitschy, trivialized construction of place. But six flags really did fly over *Los Llanos Mesteños*.

The colonizers came in waves. There were the Spanish, the French (remember the unlucky La Salle, whose Fort St. Louis was sacked by the Karankawas?), and the Spanish again. In 1821, Mexico sent the Spanish packing and gave large grants of land in the Wild Horse Desert to colonists in an effort to put boots on the ground. But fifteen years later, in 1836, the Mexican general, Santa Anna, was defeated at San Jacinto. The flag of the Texas Republic flew until 1845, when

Texas became the twenty-eighth star in the United States flag. But that lasted fewer than twenty years, and when Texas left the Union to join the South, it was the flag of the Confederacy that flew here.

In fact, Captain Mifflin Kenedy, who built La Parra Ranch, was an energetic Confederate. He did his part for the cause by moving Texas cotton through the blockade at Brownsville and shipping it to Europe out of the Mexican port of Bagdad, a town on the south side of the Rio Grande that became crucial to the Confederates' success. The cotton came back from Europe, transmuted into guns and ammunition for the Confederates, and gold for the men—Kenedy and his partner, Richard King—who masterminded the venture. Kenedy and King plowed their gold into the Wild Horse Desert, buying up and otherwise gaining control over all the Spanish and Mexican land grants that they could get their hands on. Their methods, often backed with raw muscle and firepower, were controversial. But they created the two largest, and arguably the most famous, ranches in the United States.

It took a peculiar kind of alchemy to turn cotton to gold and gold to land and land to a place in the history books.

And although this is all in the past, it is also in the present, for each of the nation-states that possessed or attempted to possess this place has left its mark. Not indelibly perhaps, but it is there.

Breathing out, this is now.

AFTER I'VE GONE SOME DISTANCE, I realize that the meandering track I am following has a destination after all. In a circuitous way, it has brought me to the Cowboy Cemetery, *El Campo Santo*, the Holy Field, as it is known to the families whose loved ones lie here. *Breathing out, I have arrived.*

An acre or so in size, the cemetery occupies a low knoll, fenced and neatly mowed, a green sanctuary embraced by the thorny wilderness of *Los Llanos Mesteños*. A few of the more recent gravesites are marked with pots filled with red plastic geraniums and unnaturally blue and purple flowers. As I pause at the gate, I hear a mourning dove, perched in a mustang grapevine draped over a tree. Gray as a ghost, a shadowy spirit, the melancholy dove asks, "*Whoo-whooo whoo-who-whooo?*"

Texas lore has it that when you hear a mourning dove asking this question near a house, someone will die. Someone has died and been buried here. Who? Cowboys? Yes. But not the kind of cowboys who worked on ranches farther west, following the seasonal work of calving, branding, herding, trailing to market. Not the kind of cowboys I saw in B westerns when I was a kid, who rode into town to blow two months' pay on a weeklong drunk and a dance hall girl before drifting on.

The cowboys whose bodies are buried here—and whose spirits surely linger about this place—are vaqueros, descendents of the Mexican-Indians who worked with the horses and cattle that the Spanish conquistadors brought to New Spain some four centuries ago. They are *Kenedeños*, the Mexican ranch workers in the employ of Captain Mifflin Kenedy, and then his son, Don Gregorio, and finally his granddaughter, Sarita. In many ways, the story of this place is their story even more than it is the story of the Kenedy family, although the Kenedys are the ones who've gotten all the attention over the years.

The vaqueros, like the Karankawas, were virtually invisible to the outside world, living here on this remote ranch year after difficult year, tending to the cattle and the horses and this land, marrying and rearing children who would carry on the same work, dying here, and resting here at last in *El Campo Santo*, a place made holy by their labor and their love. In its heyday, the ranch employed close to three hundred people; over time, it might have employed a thousand. But it's impossible to know just how many graves are here. Many are unmarked, gently rounded mounds of earth, scattered irregularly about the field. And it is not just the cowboys who are buried here, but also their wives and children and their children's children.

I walk among the headstones, considering. The oldest appears to be that of Fabia Reojas, who lived from 1810–1895, eighty-five years, a long life for that hard-working era. The names I can read are all Spanish—Rodriguez, Salazar, Estrada, Salinas, Garcia, Maldonado, Castillo—except for Isaac Hodges, who was born in Macon, Georgia, and died at La Parra Ranch, May 18, 1910. How did Isaac find his way here? Was he a cowboy? What's his story? I wish I knew, but like the Karankawas, these people are voiceless, silent. Like the doves, they are ghosts, spirits of the place.

The *Kenedeños* had it better than the Karankawas, and better than many, maybe most, cowboys in the American West. La Parra's work was hard and dangerous, but it was reliable and year-round. The paychecks weren't large, but they were regular. The cowboys had roofs over their heads, their wives had corn for their tortillas, and their younger children could go to school near their homes. Their language was the working language of the ranch, and their skills, expertise, and experience were valued. Without the vaqueros' expert knowledge of cattle and horses, there wouldn't have been a ranch.

And without the women, the vaqueros themselves could not have stayed here, for it was the family that gave them their strength. Their wives chopped the wood and milked the cows and fed the chickens and tended the gardens and disciplined the children. Women ground the corn and made the tortillas and cooked the beans and rice and stewed the beef. They sewed the family's clothes and washed them by hand with the lye soap they made themselves. They saw to the family's prayers and decorated the family's *altarcito* with flowers, candles, and images of the saints. They doctored the sick with herbs they gathered from the desert and the garden—cenizo for chills and fever, mint and manzanilla for stomach upsets, rosemary for colic, estafiate for women's disorders—and used kerosene to treat everything from colds to snakebite. Babies were born at home, the births overseen by the *parteras*, the midwives. People died at home, too, and the bodies were prepared for burial by the women, and laid out with candles and flowers, while some women said the rosary and others served sweet bread and coffee.

But the vaqueros and their families are gone. Ranchers in the Wild Horse Desert have less interest in beef than in oil these days, and pickup trucks and helicopters have replaced the working horse. While a few *Kenedeños* still live in the village of Sarita, the enclaved way of life on the ranch has come to an end.

I walk back through the cemetery to the trail. As I do, I see the unmistakable silver leaves of estafiate, known to European herbalists as artemisia, named for the goddess of the moon and the patroness, *la patrona*, of all things free, all things wild. I think: perhaps this estafiate was brought here in a bouquet to honor the dead, free at last of their mortal concerns. I take a sprig, as a reminder of women and men and children who lie, silent and solitary, in this wilderness, in the wild heart of *Los Llanos Mesteños*.

Breathing out, I am free.

LA PARRA WASN'T THE FIRST of Mifflin Kenedy's ranches in this arid region—and certainly not the first of his business endeavors. By report a quiet and deliberate man, he seems to have been gifted with the alchemical ability to turn something good into something even better. Born in 1818 to Pennsylvania Quaker parents, Kenedy was first employed (at fifteen) as a Quaker schoolteacher, then a cabin boy on a ship bound for the Orient, then a schoolteacher and a brickyard worker. Then he turned to riverboating, working his way up from clerk to captain to owner in just a decade. When the Mexican War broke out in 1848, he sailed *The Corvette* from New Orleans to the Rio Grande, where he contracted with the U.S. Army to transport troops and supplies upriver for General Zachary Taylor during the Mexican-American War. He was just thirty years old.

In 1850, Kenedy and Richard King became partners in a new steamship business, M. Kenedy and Company, using innovative, shallow-bottomed side-wheelers capable of navigating the shifting Rio Grande. The enterprise was a rip-roaring success, and by the time Texas joined the Confederacy in 1861 Kenedy and King owned more than twenty-five boats. They spent the war years working for the South. It was a costly allegiance, for when Union troops occupied Brownsville, Kenedy's property was confiscated.

But between the wars, Kenedy and King had developed an interest in ranching. The river men turned their eyes toward the limitless stretches of empty land north of the Rio Grande: the Wild Horse Desert, sometimes called by locals *El Desierto de los Muertos*, the Desert of the Dead—an ominous but fitting description. The region, also known as the Nueces Strip, had an ominous reputation, too.

The land between the Nueces River to the north and the Rio Grande to the south was truly wild and lawless. It was the focus of a border dispute between the United States and Mexico that didn't end when the 1848 Treaty of Guadalupe Hidalgo settled the southern boundary of Texas at the Rio Grande. To ranch in the Nueces Strip was to risk life and livestock, if not at the hands of the fierce Comanches and Apaches riding in from the west, then at the hands of outlaws, American and Mexican, who sometimes masqueraded as Indians. It wasn't the land the Indians and outlaws wanted, of course. They were after those innumerable, free-for-the-taking longhorns and mustangs, *los mesteños*. Few were branded; none were fenced. Many rancheros and their vaqueros were killed, and those who escaped with their lives abandoned the land and headed for safer territories.

By the 1850s, this abandoned land was becoming available, and at bargain basement prices—if clear title could be somehow obtained (under the circumstances, a Texas-sized *if*). Undaunted by the risks and eager to cash in on this bonanza, Kenedy and King became co-owners of the huge Santa Gertrudis Ranch, southwest of Corpus Christi, on the northern reaches of the Wild Horse Desert. To stock the ranch, King rode to Cruillas, Tamaulipas, in northern Mexico to buy a herd of drought-starved cattle and horses. To solve the labor problem, he also brought back the entire village of vaqueros and their families. Jane Monday and Frances Vick describe the scene: ". . . more than one hundred men, women, and children with all their possessions piled on yoked oxen, donkeys, and carts started north to the Wild Horse Desert and their new home. They brought their poultry, dogs, and pots and pans." These skilled *Kineños*, King's men, made all the difference. It was their skill and experience that made the ranch a success.

By the time the Kenedy-King partnership ended in 1868, the ranch extended from one end of *El Desierto de los Muertos* to the other, or very nearly. The two men, still friends, split their holdings, and Kenedy bought the huge Los Laureles Ranch, twenty miles south of Corpus Christi. He moved his share of the Santa Gertrudis horses and cattle to Laureles. The next year, he and his Mexican wife Petra moved to the ranch, joining the vaqueros he had hired to manage the stock.

Kenedy needed those vaqueros. To protect his cows and horses from the marauding rustlers who still plagued the Wild Horse Desert, he put the *Kenedeños* to work fencing more than one hundred and thirty thousand acres of Laureles, enclosing it with some thirty-six miles of smooth wire fence, a precursor to the more effective barbwire. (Fencing was something new, especially on this scale, for barbwire had not yet transformed the open plains into bastions of private property.) Both Kenedy and King hired and armed militias to deal with outlaws, or those they considered outlaws, which might not have been the same thing. By 1875, things had gotten to such a desperate pass that a group of Texas Rangers, led by Leander H. McNelly, was called in to restore order. It was a bloody business, but when McNelly's Rangers were finished, *El Desierto de los Muertos* was quieter, and the Rangers had earned a reputation for getting the job done.

In 1882, when Petra's health declined, Kenedy sold Laureles to a Scottish cattle syndicate for a million dollars. He built a house, a mansion with a sixty-five-foot tower, in Corpus Christi. He also purchased the four hundred thousand–acre La Parra Ranch, on the south side of Baffin Bay—the land that includes what is now Lebh Shomea. He fenced La Parra with posts brought in from Louisiana. And he and his son John—whom everyone called Don Gregorio—built the house that looked like a riverboat, or maybe a Southern plantation house, on the sand dune that is now the site of *La Casa Grande*.

Mifflin Kenedy died in 1895. But he's not buried in the Cowboy Cemetery where lie Reojas, Rodriguez, Salazar, Estrada, Salinas, Garcia, Maldonado, Castillo, and Isaac Hodges. He's not even buried in the family cemetery where the following two generations of Kenedys lie. *El Patron* is buried beside his wife in Brownsville, in the town where he first looked northward to the Wild Horse Desert and imagined owning a ranch.

That's not the end of the story, of course. But Father Kelly is tolling the *Angelus* on *El Patron*'s riverboat bell. It's time to head back to the Big House for the noon meal.

CHAPTER FOURTEEN

Plains Fare

"Eating is an agricultural act," as Wendell Berry famously said. It is also an ecological act, and a political act, too. Though much has been done to obscure this simple fact, how and what we eat determines to a great extent the use we make of the world, and what is to become of it.

MICHAEL POLLAN, *THE OMNIVORE'S DILEMMA*

To pay attention, this is our endless and proper work.

MARY OLIVER, "YES! NO!"

July 10, 1991. Eating here is much, much different from eating at home. At home, we eat and talk, eat and watch TV, eat and read. Before I know it, the food's gone. I don't remember eating it, don't remember what it tasted like—a shame, when I think of the effort that goes into growing and preparing it. Eating here, we just eat. That's all. Slowly, paying attention to each bite, each bit of food, the colors, the textures, the tastes. What would happen if I ate like this at home?

September 19, 1993. It's the absence of talk at mealtime that makes the biggest difference. There's nothing to distract me, no socializing, no inconsequential chit-chat, so the food becomes important, significant, meaning-full. No distraction and no rush, no hurry, no need to be somewhere else, do something else.

November 10, 1994. Here's what I appreciate about the food at Lebh Shomea: there's no effort at novelty, no contrivance, no artifice, no effort to make the food look like something it isn't, or to "present" it in anything other than its honest, natural form. The food is food. It's what it is, that's all it is, no more, no less. And that's enough.

THE MIDDAY MEAL is the one hot meal of the day here at Lebh Shomea, as it was on my grandparents' farm, as it would be on a working ranch. There's always plenty of food on the table, plain fare, never fancy, but hot, tasty, filling. We pick up our plates, tableware, and paper napkins and line up to serve ourselves.

Tacos are the main dish today. We assemble them at the table from crisp corn tortillas, ground beef cooked with onions and garlic, pinto beans, chopped tomatoes, raw sliced onions, and grated cheese. That, with salad (lettuce, more tomatoes, raw cauliflower and broccoli, more onions, croutons), ice cream, chocolate cookies, and iced tea or coffee, makes up the meal. It's enough. Enough, and then some.

There are a dozen of us today—eight guests, joined by three or four men who are working on the place. You can tell us apart by our costumes: guests wear leisure clothes, jeans, skirts, or Bermuda shorts. Workers, intimately acquainted with the hazards of the thorny wilderness, wear wide-brimmed hats, long-sleeved shirts, and khaki or twill pants. The workers share our silence, but they eat in the alcove off the dining room, although I know of no rule that divides us, guests and workers, in this way. The workers offer a silent prayer, cross themselves, then eat fast and leave, gathering in a shady spot near the white stucco garage where they can talk.

The rest of us say whatever form of grace is our practice, silently, then eat slowly, not having somewhere to go, or perhaps praying as we eat, or meditating, or just paying attention to our food.

Thich Nhat Hanh, in *The Miracle of Mindfulness*, reminds us how much we miss when we fail to pay attention to our food. We eat mindlessly, he says, hurriedly, inattentively, absent-mindedly. (He doesn't say that our habit of gobbling our food may have led to the nationwide epidemic of obesity or to the burgeoning sales of heartburn medication, but I think it's possible. That, and our use of food for purposes other than feeding our bodies. Using food to fill the empty places in our lives, for instance.) He invites us to practice mindful eating by paying careful attention to each bite, tasting it, being mindful of what we are doing, which is the opposite of absent-mindedness.[1]

Before Bill and I were married, I volunteered to help cook the midday neighborhood meal sponsored by the Buddhist Center in South Austin. The kitchen was always full of cheerful cooks and wonderful fresh vegetables and fruits, as well as love and laughter and friendship. Cooking and eating there—always mindfully, no matter how much noise there was, or how many children ran through the dining room, or who came or who went—was a spiritual experience that's lingered with me for decades. I learned how to organize a satisfying meal for fifteen or twenty people around whatever happened to be on the shelves in the larder, or what people brought. I learned how to make a rich, sturdy vegetable stock—no small achievement. Thoughtfully, observantly chopping carrots, celery, onions, kale, bok choy, cabbage, tomatoes, squash of all kinds—beautiful vegetables, dewed with freshness, some grown organically in the Austin community gardens—I learned a new appreciation for the remarkably varied vegetable kingdom, for all food, really.

I think of this today, as I eat the taco, the salad, the cookies, slowly, mindfully, paying attention to what I am tasting, aware of how it looks, how it smells, what it's made of, where it came from, whose hands prepared it (as far as I know), how I feel about it. Do I like the taste? What of the texture? Is it filling? Is it healthful? I consider the elements that have been joined together to make up this food: earth, air, fire, water. And when my plate is empty, I look at it, and feel a sense of gratitude.

I once heard a rabbi offer a blessing from the Torah. *V'achalta v'savata u'vayrachta.* And you shall eat and you shall be satisfied and you shall bless.

I am here, this is now. I dwell in the Ultimate.

It is grace, and grace enough.

THERE ARE PLENTY OF OPTIONS for vegetarians at Lebh Shomea. The beans are cooked without meat, and there's rice, pasta, and an abundance of vegetables, steamed, grilled, raw. A glass bowl is filled with fresh fruit—apples, bananas, oranges, grapefruit—and canned peaches, pineapple, and applesauce make frequent appearances. The desserts are tasty: pies, apple crisp, cake. There's commercial ice cream, if dairy is on your menu.

There is almost always animal protein on the table, too, sometimes baked fish, occasionally chicken or pork. But mostly beef. The steer whose flesh fills my taco was born at La Parra ranch and pastured under the South Texas sun on seacoast and King Ranch bluestem, cordgrasses, and marsh millet. He was slaughtered at the ranch and his carcass was hung in the kitchen's walk-in cooler, carved into appropriate cuts by the kitchen workers, and cooked. Today, he is the ground beef in my taco.

Having consciously chosen to eat this animal, I am glad that he grew up in the neighborhood and strolled around eating grass in the silence and solitude of this beautiful place for his entire life. I am glad he wasn't shipped to a feedlot, where he'd be jammed in with other steers and spend the last six months of his life getting as fat as possible, as fast as possible, on a diet of corn, beef tallow, molasses, and urea.

There's an interesting irony here. When you get right down to it, beef is oil—most beef, that is, present company, the steer on my plate, excepted. As Michael Pollan points out in *The Omnivore's Dilemma*, it takes about thirty-five gallons of oil, nearly a barrel, to grow enough corn to feed a steer to his market weight of twelve hundred pounds. Then there's the oil required to truck him to the feedlot, and the oil needed to produce the corn, molasses, and other fattening agents, and the oil to take him, prettily wrapped in oil-based plastic packaging, to the supermarket.

And oil is one of the other products of the Kenedy land—the major product, actually, since oil pumps far more profit than cows do. In the 1950s, the discovery of oil on Sarita's San Pablo Ranch, in Jim Hogg County, made her rich, unspeakably, enormously rich. It also brought out the greed in people, in her relatives, in her banker, in all those who were out to get a piece of her wealth.

"I feel like a sick heifer," she said to a friend, "and all those vultures are just waiting for me to die."

Here at the top of the food chain, we are what we eat.

ONCE, AT ONE OF the Sunday dinners when we are permitted to talk, a man who helped in the kitchen at Lebh Shomea remarked that we were temporarily out of beef. Over the coming week, we would be eating nilgai. A woman exclaimed, in horrified tones, "Oh, dear Lord, surely not those beautiful animals I saw in the woods!" As she forked a largish bite of roast beef into her mouth, I wondered what she thought she was eating—or if she was thinking about it at all. Cows are beautiful animals, too. It was one of those moments when I would have preferred the Rule of Silence.

Nilgai are exotic game, large Asian antelopes that were introduced to La Parra in the 1940s and thenceforth and thereafter followed God's injunction to be fruitful and multiply. They are hunted on one hundred and ninety thousand acres of the surrounding ranch (but not in the sanctuary that is Lebh Shomea), as are the native white-tailed deer, javelina, quail, turkey, dove, ducks, and geese. The ranch, owned by the Kenedy Memorial Foundation, offers annual hunting leases that start (for individual season-long memberships) at $25,000. Sounds pricey to me, although it's competitive with other leases in the area. For that, you can take away two big white-tailed bucks, a pair of does, ten nilgai, ten feral hogs, a pair of javelina, and a trio of wild turkeys, plus the daily legal limit of dove, waterfowl, and fish—which (if my math is correct) comes to $862.07 per kill, not counting the unlimited squirrels and birds you can bag. And not counting the cost of your equipment, ammunition, camp food, and travel.

It's not just hunting that's popular on the Wild Horse Desert, however. There's fishing in the waters of Baffin Bay and the Laguna Madre—redfish, black drum, speckled trout, sand trout, sea bass, flounder, sheepshead, gafftop. And in the shallow waters, you'll find shellfish, clams, mussels, and oysters, although you may have to check for current human-caused conditions (algae bloom, fertilizer drift, chemical contamination) that might render the shellfish inedible. Oh, and you may also hunt alligators, in season and on private land, if that's your fancy.

I bring this up because it is so often said that the Wild Horse Desert is a desolate place that provided almost no sustenance for its nomadic natives and the Spanish and Anglo people who came to live here. Newspapers of the 1860s widely reported the remark of General Philip Sheridan, who was dispatched to the Wild Horse Desert in the last days of the Civil War: "If I owned both hell and Texas, I'd rent out Texas and live in hell." He is said to have added that maybe the United States should go to war with Mexico again, to make her take back the Nueces Strip. (This is the same Phil Sheridan, commander of the Armies of the West, who exterminated the bison, so you know where his heart lay.) More recently, a prominent Texas food historian has asserted that the native tribes of this area survived "on precious little water and the meager food offerings of the desert."

But the food offerings of the Wild Horse Desert were anything but meager, if you knew where to look. The hunting, fishing, and foraging in pre-European days could only have been better than it is now—and according to the ranchers who are selling hunting leases, it's very, very good now. True, there were no nilgai, but there were bison, although they were never as plentiful here as they were on the plains. And while the indigenous Indians may have lacked the fire power of big-game rifles with telescopic sights, they possessed their red cedar bows, flint-tipped spears, and fish traps of woven reed: tools they made themselves and wielded with a strength and skill that most occasional sportsmen lack.

But above all, what the native peoples possessed was an earned and inherited wisdom of place that allowed them to rely on the land for all their food.

They knew when and where food would be available and how much. For them, the Wild Horse Desert was a remarkable and abundant landscape. Yes, it is hot, and yes, the sun will scorch, if you're fool enough not to wear a hat and a long-sleeved shirt when you go outside. But the descriptions of this place as sterile, unfruitful, and barren are stories told by people who were looking for the foods they understood and desired. Their vision limited by their habits, they failed to recognize the rich and varied foods that already existed here, known and available to the Indians who called this desert home.

THE PEOPLE WHO CAME after the Indians were the Spanish, the Mexicans, and the vaqueros, and the foods and food preparations they brought eventually resulted in that agreeable twentieth-century food phenomenon we call "Tex-Mex," one of America's most popular regional cuisines.

On the table at Lebh Shomea, we find plenty of simple dishes that have this Tex-Mex flavor: tacos, tortillas, enchiladas, fajitas, chile, and *refritos frijoles* (refried beans, which are not re-fried at all, but stewed and then fried). If you want more heat, there are bowls of hot salsa.

Mifflin Kenedy's Mexican wife, Petra Vela (the two were married in Brownsville in 1854) would have put these Mexican foods (or their precursors) on the Kenedy table. For breakfast at the ranch, Señora Kenedy's cook and kitchen helpers would have served such traditional dishes as *machacado con huevo* (dried beef with scrambled eggs); *chorizo* (Spanish sausage made with chile peppers); and, on festive occasions, *menudo* (spicy tripe soup topped with chopped Mexican oregano).

Dinner might have included *sopa de ajo* (garlic soup); *sopa de arroz* (traditional Mexican rice, cooked with tomato, garlic, and cumin); steamed or grilled or roasted vegetables, especially squash; beef or *cabrito* (kid goat); *lomo en adobo* (pork loin in a chile pepper sauce); *nopalitos* (prickly pear pads, peeled, diced, cooked, and served as a vegetable or salad); and *calabacitas* (made with summer squash and green chiles)—and tortillas, of course: *tortillas de trigo* (flour tortillas) and *tortillas de maíz* (corn tortillas). A typical cheese was *queso fresco*, made using the fourth stomach (*cuajo*) of a goat or calf, which contained digestive enzymes that curdled cow's milk or goat's milk. The curds were tied up in cheesecloth and hung to drain. If *cuajo* was not available, the berries of the silver-leaf nightshade might be used.

For dessert, the Kenedys might have enjoyed *churros* (Spanish cinnamon fritters) or *sopaipillas* (Mexican fritters flavored with whiskey and filled with meringue); *empanadas de camote* (sweet potato turnovers); *turcos* (baked sweet pies filled with minced pork, nuts, and raisins); or *flan* (baked caramel custard). And of course, there would have been chocolate to drink, the miraculous Aztec concoction that Hernán Cortés took back to Spain after his conquest.

With a few exceptions (chocolate, sugar, coffee, tea, whiskey), most of the foods on the ranch table were locally produced, and even the staple dried beans, corn, and rice would likely have been grown within a hundred miles. Sweet corn, tomatoes, tomatillos, and chile peppers, fresh or dried, were an essential part of every Mexican meal. Fresh or dried culinary herbs would have included epazote and cilantro—and Mexican oregano: *Poliomintha longiflora, Lippia graveolens,* and *Monarda fistulosa* var. *menthifolia* all go by that common name.

Corn, or maize, originated in the Andes and quickly traveled up-continent to Mexico, where it served as both food and money and played an important role in the Aztecs' religious practice. They believed that humans were made of maize dough, or *masa* (yes, you are what you eat), and worshipped it as a god. Corn rapidly made its way to North America and was adopted by all the native peoples who could grow it or trade for it.

But European settlers were accustomed to wheat, which they considered a more civilized food. For them, corn was a commodity: it was what you fed to your cattle or hogs or poultry. "In frontier America, as in colonial America," writes Betty Fussell, in *The Story of Corn,* "any form of bread made with corn instead of wheat was the sad paste of despair." (In our own time, we are opening yet another chapter in the transformation of corn from sacred food to commodity. It has become a fuel.)

If Europeans held the New World corn in a lower regard, they were downright suspicious of the tomatoes, tomatillos, and chile peppers brought by Columbus and other explorers from the New World. These plants are all members of the *Solanaceae,* the nightshade family, some of them poisonous, most associated with witchcraft. Chile peppers caught on fast in Europe because they were a welcome substitute for costly black pepper (which was, after all, among the things Columbus was looking for when he bumped into North America). But the tomato was accepted only in Italy, where it was thought to be an aphrodisiac, and was eaten primarily by the poor until the middle of the eighteenth century. In America, Thomas Jefferson planted tomatoes as a novelty in his famous garden, but they were not widely grown for food until after the Civil War. My mother, born in 1909, could remember being warned by older relatives that tomatoes were poisonous.

When the vaqueros and their families came to *Los Llanos Mesteños,* they cooked over an open fire, usually built in a pit. (Indoor cooking in such a hot climate is not at all comfortable.) Mesquite was favored for the fire, as it still is. Meat—beef, usually, or venison, javelina, or rabbit—was grilled or roasted on a spit or stewed in a large iron pot, as were beans and rice. Corn tortillas were made daily; *pan de campo*, or camp bread, was baked in a Dutch oven placed in the coals. Beef jerky (the word originally comes from the Incan word for dried meat, *charqui*) was made by drying sliced, salted meat, sometimes seasoned with vinegar or spices, to be eaten while working, or when fresh meat was not available.

These are simple foods, slow foods: cooking beans in a cast-iron pot hung over a mesquite fire will teach you lessons in patience. But by and large, Plains fare was healthy, with a surprising variety, and was based on what was locally (and hence readily and cheaply) available. It's a long way from our modern American diet, which is driven by food fads and fueled by the food industry rather than by stable and deeply rooted cultural traditions of food and eating. But the obtaining of food, its preparation, and its consumption is at the heart of our relationship with the natural world. When we fail to understand this, we're in trouble.

I RISE FROM THE dining room table. Others are still eating and I feel apologetic when the scrape of my chair breaks the silence. I replace the chair and wipe off my table mat, then carry my plate and tableware to the appropriate bins. I pause beside the glass bowl of fruit on the way out the door. Apples, bananas, and oranges. I wonder if I have room.

Later, I decide. Maybe later, when I'm hungry again.

V'achalta v'savata u'vayrachta. And you shall eat and you shall be satisfied and you shall bless.

CHAPTER FIFTEEN

Storms

We think of monks as being remote from the world, but Saint Benedict, writing in the sixth century, notes that a monastery is never without guests, and admonishes monks to "receive all guests as Christ." . . . A story said to originate in a Russian Orthodox monastery has an older monk telling a younger one: "I have finally learned to accept people as they are. Whatever they are in the world, a prostitute, a prime minister, it is all the same to me. But sometimes I see a stranger coming up the road and I say, 'Oh, Jesus Christ, is it you again?'"

KATHLEEN NORRIS, *DAKOTA:*
A SPIRITUAL GEOGRAPHY

July 9, 1991. I wish wish wish I could leave home without feeling that I'm shirking some important responsibility, and stay here without feeling as if I've run away from home. Will that ever be possible? I doubt it.

September 20, 1993. The greatest blessing in being here—no distractions— is also the hardest. Each day, facing what is inside me, the disappointments, the obstinacies, the angers, the doubts, the impulsiveness, all my broken pieces. There's no getting away from them. Yet I remember the story a Buddhist teacher gave me. A man from the city sees a potter at work in a remote village. He is astonished by the graceful forms of his pots, but worried that they might be too fragile. "Oh, but you're looking at the outside," said the potter. "The form I'm after is within. What interests me is what remains when the pot is broken."

November 11, 1994. Pots smashed all over the place, a rubble of broken shards, clay dust. Is there anything inside? Anything at all?

THE GNATS ARE BACK, with a vengeance. I called Bill after lunch, from the phone in the basement of the Big House. When I reached him, he said tersely that he'd just spent an uncomfortable, apprehensive half hour huddled with the dogs and the cat in Archie Bunker—our storm shelter, a substantial cement affair dug into the ground and heaped over with dirt and vines. He was alerted by a radar image of the storm on the local television channel, and by our weather radio, which lets us know when the Weather Service posts a watch or a warning. We were lucky. The storm—was it a tornado? No word on that yet— missed Meadow Knoll by a couple of miles.

But there's a considerable amount of wind damage—things tossed around, plywood torn loose, tree branches down—and the tornado warnings haven't expired yet. It's too soon to breathe a sigh of relief. And there's flooding. Bill says that the creek is out of its banks and water is running across the meadow, lapping halfway up the hill. The house is in no danger, but water over the septic system is definitely bad news.

There's no way to keep the gnats at bay now. I should be there to give him a hand. Getting the cat and the dogs—our two black Labs both weigh in at eighty-plus pounds—into the bunker is a two-person job, not to mention all the outdoor stuff that needs to be moved under cover when we get a wind-storm. There's plenty I could do to help. No wonder Bill sounds harassed, out of breath and out of patience, as he recites the litany of weather woes.

"I wish I were there," I say. I clear my throat. "I think I should come home. If I packed up now and started right away, I could be home by seven or eight."

"No," he replies curtly. "Stay where you are. If we're going to have trouble with the septic system, one less person flushing is good. Anyway, I don't think you could get across the creek at the culvert. The road's out." He pauses, then softens his tone. "Thanks, Susan. I appreciate the offer. But I have to go now. I've got to anchor the bridge over Iris Pool before the creek takes it out."

One less person flushing.

My feelings aren't hurt, are they? Probably. No, certainly. I feel rejected, resentful. But he's right. Even if I could get home (it sounds like I can't), I'd just be in the way. There's nothing much I can do to help, except say a prayer. If I believed in prayer.

Well, a little prayer probably wouldn't hurt, so I pause to sketch out my request, add a fervent "Please," and wonder if my request will have a better chance of being heard if I cross myself. I've gone this far, I might as well go the rest of the way. I do.

When in Rome.

REFLECTING ON THE FOOD Petra Kenedy would have served her family has made me wonder about her. What kind of a woman was she? What kind of woman would follow her husband to this remote corner of the desert, to build a ranch, make a home here? I've run across the titles of a couple of books that might have some information about her, so I go upstairs to the library. I find the books, then stop at the table in the main hall of the library to glance at the newspaper. My eye is caught by a story about a traffic stop Border Patrol agents made at the Sarita checkpoint in February. They opened the trailer of an eighteen-wheeler and found seventy-eight people stuffed behind a load of auto parts. A month later, three more eighteen-wheelers, ninety-two people inside.

And in Washington, there's talk of a fence. A twelve-foot fence, which leads one border state governor to quip that it will lead to a run on thirteen-foot ladders. A fence, I think angrily, remembering the Berlin Wall, the wall the Israelis are building across the West Bank, the Great Wall of China, Hadrian's Wall. Secure the borders. Man the barricades. Repel, reject, repulse the barbarians, the aliens, the unwashed, the unwelcome, the unforgiven.

I fold up the paper and put it back on the table, take my book, and go outside. The air is oppressively muggy, and the feeling of fullness, of satisfaction, of blessedness, that buoyed me after lunch is gone. How is it that I can swing from one extreme to the other, from contentment to a savage discontent, in the space of a half hour? I came here to be quiet, to reflect, to find peace, and all I can think of at the moment is the storm at home, and the storm that swirls around this peaceful place. Border issues are serious issues, yes. But it's impossible to keep people out if they're determined to come. Is the government really going to build a fence? That's no answer. And what to do with the undocumented people who are already here? If I were in charge—

I shake my head, feeling disgusted with myself. I'd never make a monk. I have too many connections to the world.

I glance up at the clouds, still building toward the east, but darker now, and more threatening, their quilted bellies a heavy, ominous gray. Wind rustles the papery fronds of the palms like pages turning in a book. Somewhere to the south, a rain crow—the yellow-billed cuckoo—is ratcheting out an announcement of the coming storm. But there's enough of a breeze to ward off the pesky mosquitoes, and Ezekiel will be hot. Maybe I'll sit outside and read until the rain sends me indoors.

I walk across the ankle-high grass to a small concrete bench under a palm tree. A squirrel has been here before me, nibbling seeds, and has left a scattering of empty hulls. I brush them off, sit down, and begin paging through the book, looking for references to Petra Kenedy, knowing that I'll be lucky to find anything. Historians are happy to tell us in detail about the men who conquered this and founded that, but they don't have much to say about the women. More silent people, more voices lost in the solitudes of time.

"Excuse me," a sharp voice says, "but you really shouldn't be sitting there, you know."

I look up, startled. Standing on the sidewalk, some ten paces away, is the gray-haired woman who sat across from me at the noon meal. Although she's not wearing a habit, she is unmistakably a religious, her white blouse buttoned up to the neck, a gold cross, a gray calf-length skirt, black stockings, lace-up oxfords. Her hands are clasped at her waist. She is frowning.

I'm surprised that she's spoken. I put my finger on the page to mark my place and give her an inquiring look.

"You're not supposed to walk on the grass," Black Stockings says crisply. "You'll get chiggers. Ticks, too. Didn't you read the instructions?"

Really. It's all I can do to keep from rolling my eyes. But I only press my lips together, lower my head, and return pointedly to my book. With an emphatic, impatient cluck-cluck, Black Stockings stalks off, her stiff back expressing displeasure at my disobedience.

I frown uneasily. Am I breaking a rule I've never heard about? If walking across the grass really isn't a good idea, why put a bench here? I feel like a third grader chided by her teacher. And then I feel the irritation rising inside me, and all thoughts of reading go out of my head. Chiggers and ticks, really! This person doesn't give a damn about chiggers and ticks. She just wants to tell me I am breaking some silly rule.

Well, she's breaking a rule, too.

Hey, lady, didn't you notice the rule about silence? How'd you manage to miss the Big One, huh? Can't you friggin' READ?

And at that irony, I finally have to smile. I am grateful for the Rule, actually. Without it, I'm sure I would have said something I'd be sorry for later.

Still, I'm saying it in my mind. And isn't that just as toxic (to me, anyway, to my spirit) as if I had said it out loud, as if I had hurled the words like angry stones at this person who has launched the rockets of her scolding words at me?

My smile becomes a scowl. Silence isn't much good if I'm muttering through the clenched teeth of my mind, planning reciprocal warfare, a verbal arms race. The solitude is charged, now, tense, electrical. My words are suspended in it, writhing, sparking, hissing like live wires, and just as deadly. *How'd you manage to miss the Big One, huh? Can't you friggin' READ?*

A drop of rain splats onto the book—a library book—and I close it and tuck both books under my arm. If I don't go in, the book will get wet.

There's probably a rule against reading library books outside, anyway.

Resentfully, defiantly, I walk back to Ezekiel. Across the grass.

A THUNDERSTORM. Lightning, snapping, crackling, blue-bright. Sweeping tropical rain, heavy winds that sway the tops of the palms and shake out bursts of papery fans, shredding them, sending them sailing like confetti through the air. The grass and shrubs are green, the sky is green, the air is green—it's like looking through the bottom of a green bottle into an aquarium full of green plants. The javelina family, mother and four or five youngsters, seems not to mind the wet—perhaps they even enjoy its coolness on their leathery hides. But as the winds pick up and the rain sweeps across the grass like a wet broom, the deer and the turkeys seek cover in the brushy wilderness on the other side of the road, where canopies of leathery leaves will keep them dry.

It's only a thunderstorm, I know. If there was anything really serious—a hurricane stewing in the rich, hot broth of the Gulf, say—Father Kelly would post warnings on the bulletin board. If things got serious, we'd evacuate inland, to safer ground. The last hurricane, Bret, in 1999, came in just to the south of here, clocking 115 mph winds; before that, it was Allen, in 1980, which sent a twelve-foot storm surge across the barrier islands. In 1970, Celia's microbursts did enormous damage in Corpus Christi and three years before that, Beulah doused the area with torrential rains. Storms are a fact of life here on the flat coastal plains. All you can do is batten down the hatches or head for high ground.

I've closed the windows to keep the rain out, and it's steamy in Ezekiel, sweltering, despite the whirring fan, although how much of it is ordinary heat and how much is my molten temper, it's impossible to tell. I adjust the blinds so no one can look in. Why? There's nobody out there, unless Black Stockings braves the storm to peek through my window to see what other rules I'm breaking.

Well, I'll give her something to see, I chuckle grimly. I take off my tee-shirt and bra. The shirt, rinsed out in cold water, wrung out, and pulled back on, makes me shiver. I let the fan blow on me, and feel a little saner. Not much, but a little.

When I'm cool enough (this takes a while), I put my meditation bench on the floor and sit with the gnats and my raw temper for a half hour, paying attention to my breath, letting the feelings come, watching them go. There are lots of feelings. Lots and lots. Guilt for not being with Bill when he needs me. Anger—rage, really—at Black Stockings for ruining a perfectly good afternoon. Anger at myself for feeling guilty and angry, when I've come all this way to enjoy peace and quiet, silence and solitude.

One of my teachers told me a story once about G. I. Gurdjieff. An old man, a member of Gurdjieff's spiritual community, caused everybody a lot of grief, always making critical remarks, always arguing, forever refusing to do his share of the work. When he left the community, everybody was relieved. "Thank God, he's gone. Now we can have some peace around here!"

But Gurdjieff went after the man, imploring him to stay, finally even offering him a stipend if he'd come back. When the old man reappeared, everybody was upset—especially when they found out that he was actually getting paid to be there, while they had to pay. They demanded an explanation. "I brought him back," the teacher said, "because we need this man. He's yeast in our bread. He's teaching us about anger, guilt, patience, compassion."

Anger, guilt. Yeast in my bread. Can I, will I, learn patience, compassion? Patience with Black Stockings, with myself. Compassion, even? Not yet, but eventually, maybe. Maybe. But I doubt it.

Then after a while, even these questions go away and there's just the breath. Another while, and I'm okay. Well, not maybe entirely okay. But okay enough.

I wash my face, put on a dry shirt, and look out the window. It's still raining out there.

It's a good afternoon to read.

CHAPTER SIXTEEN

The Kenedy Women

Was Petra Vela Kenedy born the pampered daughter of a silver-rich governor, who bought her a Mexican colonel and then left her wealthy enough to buy a million-acre ranch for her new Anglo husband and powerful enough to become the Catholic grande dame of the new boomtown of Corpus Christi? Or, did she rise from humble beginnings on a dusty ranch in the quiet backwater of Mier, México, suffer through servitude and abandonment, and finally—as a single mother with a half-dozen children—did she fight her own way up in the war-torn world of the Rio Grande border?

ANA CAROLINA CASTILLO CRIMM,
"PETRA VELA AND THE KENEDY FAMILY LEGACY"

September 12, 1998. Reading Kathleen Norris, Dakota. *She's writing about the character of Dakotans, who are often severely tested by the isolation and remoteness of the place where they live. "Sometimes people rise to the occasion and do well more than they believe they can do at all," she says. "What good is a desert? Well, I believe a desert is where such gifts appear." I think of this, and of the unremembered women who transformed this place, this Wild Horse Desert, into a home. Of the skill it took, the effort, the devotion. Did they bring those gifts to the desert, or did the desert give them those gifts?*

May 16, 2000. I'm thinking that maybe there's a novel here, in the lives of the three women—Petra, Marie Stella, Sarita—who made this place. Their factual realities, their whole truths, those are all unknowable. But their realities can be imagined, their truths recreated, their dreams dreamed. I think of Barry Lopez, in Crossing Open Ground: *we are at our best when we no longer demand "the" truth and realize that the truths that guide our lives are metaphorical, are stories.*

A novel? An intriguing possibility. Not this year. Not next. But later. Maybe.

October 25, 2003. Was it Isak Dinesen who said, "All the sorrows of life can be borne if only we can make them into stories"?

October 27, 2003. Everything I've heard about the Wild Horse Desert puts the men at the center. Mifflin Kenedy, Richard King, the two powerful men who bought, stole, shaped, and tamed this vast, muscular stretch of coastal prairie. But that's wrong. It was the women who inhabited this place, in a deep, abiding sense. They grew and prepared the food, managed the clothing, nursed the injured, bore and reared the children. Men may conquer a place, or believe that they have. Women inhabit it.

I'M READING THE HISTORY of the Wild Horse Desert, *Los Llanos Mesteños*, *El Desierto de los Muertos*, where, as one wit put it, "Everything that grows has a thorn." Reading about the lawless Nueces Strip, the bloody Coastal Bend between the Nueces River to the north and the Rio Grande to the south, which General Sheridan thought might reasonably be returned to Mexico, since nobody on this side really wanted it.

Of course, they wanted it. Mifflin Kenedy and Richard King, that hard-driving pair lashed by the same compelling ambition, who knew that land was power, the only kind of power that meant anything in this country. That's why they took so many risks to seize it, to hang onto it, to set up cow camps and run cattle and horses here. But living here, making a home here—that was a different matter. How did they do it, those men?

But it wasn't the men. It was the women, those wives and mothers who were responsible for the household, for the family, who planted gardens and raised chickens and bore babies and buried the dead. How did they manage in those difficult days before electricity and running water and refrigerators, before storm warnings on radio and television, before women could do what I've just done: sit in a wet tee-shirt under a fan? How did Petra Kenedy—the first Kenedy woman to make a home in this place—stand the heat? Those heavy skirts, those high-necked blouses, those stiff bodices—didn't she almost smother?

PETRA VELA KENEDY

THERE ARE TWO VERSIONS of the life of Petra Kenedy. In one, she is the daughter of a Mexican landed aristocrat who brought social status, respectability, and wealth to Mifflin Kenedy. In the other, she is a "humble ranch girl" who grew up on a remote land grant tract on the south side of the Rio Grande, on Mexico's dangerous northern frontier.

The truth, as usual, involves something of both. The Vela family, originally from Catalonia in Spain, had lived in the New World for six generations. Petra's father owned nearly nine thousand acres of land in the Wild Horse Desert north of the Rio Grande, although the family, which was prosperous but not wealthy, lived in the village of Mier, just south of the Rio Grande. In 1837, when Petra was fifteen, she became the mistress of a young lieutenant in the Mexican army named Luis Vidal. In 1842, Vidal was promoted to captain and married the politically well-connected woman to whom he had been engaged for five years. But his relationship to Petra continued, and soon she had borne him eight children, five of whom lived to adulthood.

But Vidal himself died in 1849, and Petra (who had by then inherited a share of her father's estate) was independent. In 1850, she and her children moved to Brownsville. Not long after, she met and fell in love with the up-and-coming Mifflin Kenedy. To their alliance, she brought her Mexican connections and ranching background, a ranch near the Nueces River (part of her father's estate) for Mifflin to manage, and her five children. He brought strength, ambition, and a greater financial security. But not murder: there is no truth to the romantic legend, often told by the Kenedys themselves, that Petra was married to Vidal when she and Kenedy met and that Mifflin was so enamored of her that he arranged Vidal's death.

In any case, the Kenedys' first son was born in 1852. They were married in 1854, and Petra bore her husband five more children. During the Civil War, Mifflin took Petra back to his native Pennsylvania, where (according to an awed Coatesville newspaper reporter) she wore a "Spanish mantilla of black lace" with a "native grace which none of the ladies in the town dared seek to imitate." Part of her mystery, undoubtedly, was the fact that she spoke only Spanish— whether by choice or necessity is not recorded.

The marriage flourished, and Mifflin began to devote himself to buying as much of the Wild Horse Desert as he could manage. This proved to be a substantial amount. With Richard King, he bought Santa Gertrudis (203,000 acres), then Los Laureles (about 115,000 acres), and finally La Parra (400,000 acres). However Petra had begun her life, she would end it as the wife of a rancher.

But this wasn't an ordinary ranching family, isolated on the desert. In addition to the ranch houses at Los Laureles and La Parra, the Kenedys had a house in Brownsville, where Petra is remembered for her generous gifts to both church and community. And in 1885, Mifflin Kenedy built a magnificent Italianate villa on City Bluff in Corpus Christi. From all reports, it was an architectural wonder: a tower so tall that it could be seen by ships out on the bay, the exterior painted in three shades of olive green, interior panelings of walnut, oak, cherry, mahogany, and cypress, a banister of polished mesquite. A domestic wonder, too, with hot and cold running water and two hundred gas lamps.

Petra didn't live to enjoy the convenience of hot water and gas lamps or the entertainments of Corpus Christi. She died of cancer only a month after the elegant Kenedy villa was completed. But she did live to see her son John Gregory married and to meet her new daughter-in-law, Marie Stella Turcotte Kenedy, who was as French and Catholic as Petra was Mexican and Catholic.

MARIE STELLA TURCOTTE KENEDY

HERE'S WHAT I KNOW about Marie Stella, and it isn't much. John Gregory (Petra called him Don Gregorio, after her father) attended Spring Hill College in Mobile, Alabama. In March 1882, he married the sister of one of his classmates, twenty-year-old Stella Turcotte, a beautiful New Orleans belle. It was a society wedding at St. Louis Cathedral, and why not? The daughter of a prominent New Orleans merchant family was marrying the scion of one of Texas' most famous ranching families.

Mifflin Kenedy had bought La Parra earlier that same year, and Don Gregorio was to manage it. The newlyweds took up residence in a new four-bedroom frame house on the highest point of land on the ranch. They lived there for thirty-five years, until the house was hauled off and *La Casa Grande* was built in its place.

Don Gregorio and Stella also had a house in Corpus Christi (which at the time had a population of some four thousand), next door to Mifflin Kenedy's towered, olive-green villa. Previously owned by Martha Rabb, "The Cattle Queen of Texas," it was called the Magnolia Mansion. Stella's two children were born there, John (always called Johnny) in 1885 and Sarita in 1889.

With her New Orleans sophistication and her French ways (she spoke French and taught it to her children), Stella must have glittered in Corpus Christi. Indeed, the Kenedys and Kings were among the brightest stars in the little town's galaxy, and their extravagant mansions, lined up in a row on the bluff, were visible from everywhere.

But there was the ranch, and while the rancher's wife might reasonably spend at least part of the social season in town, her husband could expect her to be with him at La Parra. Don Gregorio's wife did not assume the role of *patrona*, however, as her mother-in-law Petra had so naturally done and as her daughter Sarita would do in her turn. In fact, Stella seems to have participated little in La Parra's working life. Whether she was happy is a question that cannot be answered, for there is almost no documentation of her life. But she made her mark on the ranch, and on Lebh Shomea, in ways that might not have been foreseen.

Devoutly Catholic, Stella took comfort from the frequent visits of priests—Missionary Oblates of Mary Immaculate—who traveled on horseback through *El Desierto de los Muertos*, stopping at each far-flung ranch along the way. After all, it was a French order, founded in 1816 to bring the faith to the rural peoples of France, and most of its priests were French.

The Wild Horse Desert was not France, however, and this circuit-riding mission was both difficult and dangerous. Priests died in epidemics or simply disappeared in the desert; the body of one, the "Lost Priest," wasn't found for a decade. But these dedicated men remained faithful to their calling and to the mission of their order. For many who lived in remote places, the "Cavalry of Christ," as the Oblates were known, would be their major contact with the Gospel.

For Stella, as they had been for Petra, the Oblates must have been a godsend. At the time she came to live at La Parra, Jean Breteau traveled the coastal route and always stopped at the ranch. Padre Juanito, as he was fondly called, must have brought a cheerful lift and a new energy to Stella's ranch-bound days. Perhaps they spoke French together. Perhaps he brought news from the outside world as well as spiritual counsel, or news from neighboring ranches. Whatever their relationship, it must have been important to her, for in 1897, Padre Juanito signed the dedication of the new chapel she had built, certainly with his encouragement, perhaps at his urging. Stella displayed her piety, her taste for Old World culture, and her husband's wealth by acquiring pieces of Italian baroque artwork for her new chapel: a painting attributed to Caravaggio and a copy of Sebastiano del Piombo's *Madonna and Child*.

A few years later, beside the chapel, she constructed a grotto of Our Lady of Lourdes in the cemetery where she herself would be buried. If its rough-hewn limestone bulk (limestone quarried in the Hill Country, not far from Meadow Knoll) seems out of place on this flat, featureless coastal prairie, it would not have seemed so to Stella, for Lourdes and all that it symbolized must have been a part of the landscape of her spiritual imagination and the French heritage to which she clung here in *El Desierto de los Muertos*. "I think of two landscapes," Barry Lopez writes, "one outside the self, the other within." The interior landscape, he adds, is a "projection within a person of a part of the exterior landscape."

But it works the other way around, too. Mifflin imagined a landscape of cattle and horses and vaqueros, busy and rich and productive, and fashioned the ranch in that image. Stella imagined a landscape that was cultured, European, and French, and projected that onto the desert: her chapel, her grotto, and eventually, her house. And while *La Casa Grande* might be Spanish on the outside, the elaborate interior decorations and ornate furnishings were French. Completed in 1923, it was surely designed to represent to the world her enviable social position and her cultural affiliations.

Both of Stella's children, Johnny and Sarita, had been married for some time, and it was already clear that there would be no grandchildren to carry on the Kenedy name or to occupy *La Casa Grande*. If there were any storms in Stella's placid life, they must have swirled around her children. Living in a time and place where women defined themselves chiefly in relationship to their families, she had to have felt a wrenching sense of loss when she understood that there would be no more Kenedys. What did her life signify, if there was to be no legacy, no children of her children?

The year 1925 must have been especially stormy. It was then—according to Ray Fernandez's lawsuit against the Kenedy estate—that a baby was born to Maria, a La Parra housemaid, in a home for unwed mothers in Waco. Named Ann, the child was Johnny Kenedy's daughter, the lawsuit alleges. Ann was packed off to board with a relative and her mother went back to work for the Kenedys, now in the Kenedy mansion in Corpus Christi. Two years later (1927), Maria bore another child, a boy, who is said to have died in 1931 of a mysterious food poisoning that also sickened the little girl. Foul play was suspected.

Of course, taking a mistress was as common a practice in South Texas as it was anywhere. In Mexico and throughout Central and South America, a man's wife and his "first family" lived in *la casa grande* and his mistress and her children lived in *la casa chica* (little house). A man who divided his time between his ranch and his mansion in town might even have more than one *casa chica*. Such arrangements, rarely spoken of publicly, were certainly known to the family members, although none of the Kenedys have left any record of such knowledge.

Perhaps it was around this time that Stella proposed to her daughter Sarita that since there could be no legitimate Kenedy heirs, *La Casa Grande* and the surrounding ten thousand acres should be bequeathed to the Missionary Oblates, the traveling padres who had served her spiritual needs so faithfully.

That, after all is said and done, is Stella's legacy, her impact on this land, and it is of enormous significance. Without her, what is now Lebh Shomea would have passed into other hands, and I—and the other seekers who come to this wilderness in search of silence and solitude—would not be here.

BUT THERE'S YET one more Kenedy woman.

Born to Don Gregorio and Stella Turcotte Kenedy on September 19, 1889, Sarita spent her childhood at La Parra. A tomboy, she rode with the vaqueros, learned all she could about the workings of the ranch, and began to fill the role of a young *patrona*. She went to several boarding schools and at eighteen did a couple of semesters' work at Sophie Newcomb College in New Orleans (where I would serve as dean some seventy years later). She made her debut in New Orleans, and in 1910 she married Arthur Lee East, son of a neighboring Texas rancher, in Corpus Christi Cathedral. But both Sarita and Arthur caught undulant fever. The illness is said to have made it impossible for them to have children.

Childless, Sarita East threw her substantial energies into the ranch she loved, taking on management responsibilities that might have belonged to her brother Johnny, had he been so inclined. But he was more interested in hunting and drinking than in ranching, so she carried on. As a girl, she had loved riding and roping, loved the grasslands and brush country, loved cows and horses, and now the ranch captured all her attention. In the 1930s, after the death of her father, she undertook a war against the encroaching brush in an attempt to improve the pastures and began her own breeding program to improve the cattle. "Sarita East went on the range to supervise," one of her employees said respectfully. "She was a very good rider and helped cut the cattle. She was good people."

As *patrona*, Sarita took her responsibilities seriously. Fluent in Spanish, she made sure that her three hundred ranch employees had adequate housing, education for the young children, medical care for the family, beef for the table, and all the free ammunition a man could use. At Christmas, she sent gifts: "The ladies got linens, towels, and the kids, toys," one remembered. "The men got a bonus." A nephew described her as a "cowgirl" who liked to attend her ranch-hands' weekend barbecues and join in the Texas Two-step or the Cotton-eyed Joe, a can of Pabst Blue Ribbon in her hand.

Sarita was also a charitable woman. "If somebody had a problem, they knew where to go," one of her vaqueros remembered. "She paid to get the babies born, bury the dead, and feed the hungry. She was called *madrina*—godmother—because it seemed she always had something for the children."

It was perhaps as *madrina* that Sarita found her greatest pleasure. She gave away amounts ranging from $40,000 to $100,000 a year to various worthy causes, many local, most Catholic. By the early 1950s, oil had been discovered on Sarita's San Pablo ranch, and she would undoubtedly have given that money away, too, if she'd had the cooperation of her banker, an unhelpful man known locally as *El Vibora Seca*, the "Dry Snake," who was anxious to keep her money in his bank. Eventually, the Alice National Bank would face criminal charges for its mishandling of her legacy.

But there were storms in Sarita's life, oh, yes, there were storms. Cruelly, *la madrina* could not bear children. Her husband, Arthur, was rumored to be unfaithful. There may or may not have been that affair between her brother and the housemaid. And then her father died, leaving her with the care of both her invalid mother and the ranch. That was in 1931. Her mother died in 1940, her husband in 1944, her brother in 1948. She buried them all in an orderly row in the family cemetery, near the grotto and under the benevolent gaze of the Blessed Mother, Our Lady of Lourdes. She left a space between her mother and Arthur. That was where she would be buried.

The emptiness of the huge house must have echoed in Sarita's bones as she contemplated the long, vacant years, alone. Most of her friends and cousins lived at distances that made frequent visits difficult. What was there to look forward to but more of the same silence and solitude, day after day? Who could blame her if, like her brother, she developed a fondness for Scotch?

And then—just as it had happened with her mother—a cleric came along to brighten her life, lift her spirits, and give her a sense of purpose. His name was Brother Leo. He was a young monk, and quite good-looking. He was traveling on a mission for the Trappists, having been charged by his abbot to raise funds for various monastic projects. Sarita, 59, and Leo, 31, hit it off. Some people have called it a love story; "she was obviously in love with him," said Francis Verstraeten, who hosted the pair during the first of their trips to Argentina to visit fledgling Trappist projects. Brother Leo called it "our special relationship"— perhaps Sarita was the mother he'd never had and he the son Sarita could not bear. Whatever the nature of their friendship, the young monk would play an increasingly important role in helping this wealthy woman expand her charitable giving during the remaining thirteen years of her life.

In October 1959, he invited Sarita to visit Argentina with him. In early January 1960, he introduced her to Peter Grace, a New York financier and Trappist supporter who helped her set up a foundation as a vehicle for increased giving. Within a few weeks of that meeting, she had rewritten the will she made at the death of her brother in 1948, reducing the shares she'd planned to give to the Diocese of Corpus Christi and to family members in favor of a new foundation named for her mother and father. La Parra, she thought, ought to go to the Trappists, rather than the Oblate Fathers, an idea that Brother Leo did not greet with enthusiasm. He was apparently not attracted by the notion of living in the heat and isolation of the Wild Horse Desert. In the new scheme of things, the Oblates were to keep the La Parra headquarters and the surrounding 10,000 acres, but lose the mineral rights.

The creation of the foundation was complicated by the intervention of *El Vibora Seca*, who raised one objection after another, some of them valid. But things went along more or less swimmingly until late in 1960, when, during a visit to the Argentine project, Sarita was diagnosed with inoperable cancer. She died a few months later in a New York hospital. She was buried between her mother and her husband, under the loving gaze of Our Lady of Grace, beside the chapel her mother had built with the encouragement of Padre Juanito.

That's when the storms really began, howling winds, manic rains, a titanic surge. There were loud charges leveled against Brother Leo and Peter Grace for exerting undue influence upon an impressionable older lady. There were appeals to the Vatican to settle the disagreements between the Corpus Christi Diocese and the Trappists. There was even an investigation by the Texas Attorney General of the Alice National Bank, which controlled Sarita's foundation.

It was generally agreed that the Oblates should receive what they now possess, since they were named in all four of Sarita's wills. But more than 180 family claimants, including descendents of her Mexican grandmother Petra, emerged to challenge the 1960 will. Over the next few decades, these disputes were eventually settled. In 2001, the last of those claims was denied: that Don Gregorio had not adequately compensated Mifflin Kenedy's legally adopted Mexican daughter, Carmen, for her share of Mifflin's estate. (It is speculated that Carmen was a daughter born out of wedlock before Mifflin and Petra were married.) The 2002 Fernandez paternity suit, still outstanding, looks as if it will enjoy a long run in the Texas courts.

Also likely to be around for a while is a recent claim by the descendents of a Mexican landowner that some 363,000 acres of land in the Wild Horse Desert was merely leased to Mifflin Kenedy, not sold, as has always been claimed. The family wants the land—and compensation for the oil taken from it. "At its core," says the *New York Times*, "the issue turns on an interpretation of history: Were the great Texas ranchers like Mr. Kenedy and Richard King, of the fabled King Ranch, visionary figures who tamed a wasteland with honor and grit, or were they Anglo land grabbers who used trickery and violence to rob Mexicans of their property?"

Which interior landscape did they project onto the exterior world?

Sarita's story, the last chapter in the long-running saga of the Kenedys and their vast landscapes, interior and exterior, does not appear to have ended.

I PUT MY READING ASIDE and go to the window. It's nearly time for supper. The storm has passed, the wind has died down, but the sky is gray and it is still raining—the kind of slow, steady rain that soaks into thirsty soil, feeding the roots of grasses and trees, comforting the animals, renewing life in this place.

But what is this place, exactly? Is it Karankawa country, New Spain, Mexico or Tejas or Texas, the Wild Horse Desert, *El Desierto de los Muertos*, the Nueces Strip, La Parra Ranch, or Lebh Shomea? Is it all of these, or one of these, or some or none of these? Each name reflects a different landscape, a different sort of land, a different human perception of how the land and its resources should be used, a different projection of an interior landscape onto the exterior world. Each name tells a different story, triumphant and tragic, heroic and mischievous, stories of perseverance and piety and power and undisguised, undisguisable greed. True grit, or true greed? Hard work and honest industry, or tricks and thievery?

But Father Kelly is ringing Mifflin Kenedy's riverboat bell, tolling the *Angelus*. I look across the way and see him bent to his meditative task, praying with strong, regular pulls. It's time for supper.

I drape my poncho over my head and set out through the rain.

CHAPTER SEVENTEEN

Belonging to the Community of the Land

We can change places, move, but this is still to look for a place, for this we
need as a base to set down Being and to realize our possibilities—a here
from which the world discloses itself, a there to which we can go.

ERIC DARDEL

We abuse land because we regard it as a commodity belonging to us.
When we see land as a community to which we belong, we may begin
to use it with love and respect. . . . That land is a community is the
basic concept of ecology, but that land is to be loved and respected is
an extension of ethics. That land yields a cultural harvest is a fact long
known, but latterly often forgotten.

ALDO LEOPOLD, *SAND COUNTY ALMANAC*

April 14, 1995. Reading David Steindl-Rast, A Listening Heart: *"To be present where we are means to wake up to this place." Which means waking up not just to its present, but also to its past and its future. And staying awake long enough to feel a kind of reciprocal energy: I am placed, in the present, in this place, here. Grounded. Rooted. Landmarked.*

August 1, 2001. Scott Sanders writes: "We need a richer vocabulary of place." Yes. I need a clearer language to describe where I am, so I can know who I am. I need to know the boundaries of my place, need to know the plants and animals and people who share it with me. Without that knowing, I might as well be anyplace. Without it, I am placeless.

July 15, 2007. I recently met the naturalist-writer Susan Tweit, who blogs and writes about the "community of the land," a phrase first used by Aldo Leopold. Susan uses the phrase in place of the word "nature," she says, because "nature" implies something other, alien, separate from humans. But landscape is not "out there," beyond, apart. We shape the land, the land shapes us, in an infinitely interactive way. Yes, a community. But I fear that we humans are not good neighbors.

AFTER SUPPER (the usual cold cuts and cheese for sandwiches, salad, cottage cheese, fruit, and coffee), I call Bill. It has stopped raining there, although the creek is still out of its banks, the road is an axle-deep quagmire and the septic field flooded (no flushing). He sounds much better, though, almost happy.

"We have a new bull," he announces cheerfully.

"A new bull?" I'm perplexed. We have two cows, but livestock breeding is not something we have discussed. I am no *partera*. Bovine midwifery is not on the list of skills I hope to achieve in this lifetime.

"Yeah. A great white bull. I'm calling him Moby." Bill chuckles. "Moby's a whole lotta bull, I'll tell you. Weighs a couple of thousand pounds, at least. He's chowing down on the Johnson grass." He chuckles again. "*Cojones muy grandes!*"

It turns out that Moby Bull is a Charolais, bred by the French since the sixteenth century as meat, milk, and draft animals. And he doesn't belong to us, I am relieved to learn. That is, we have him only temporarily, until his owner can be located—we hope. Moby showed up in one of our pastures, Bill reports, amorously eyeing Blossom—our longhorn-Limousin heifer—over the fence. Blossom, who in our opinion is too young for that sort of hanky-panky, went on with her grazing in a don't-bother-me way, although Bill says she cast occasional flirtatious glances and flicked her tail provocatively.

"I hope you can locate Moby's owner fast," I say worriedly. "Two thousand pounds of bull with love on his mind won't be stopped by five strands of barbwire. And we don't want a calf this year. Do we?"

Bill agrees. He has already put up a sign in the post office and made a call to the sheriff's office, which is about all he can do. Put up a sign and wait.

Wild animals go anywhere they please, but domestic animals are supposed to stay put. It's a community rule, agreed to as a way of keeping the peace. The animals don't pay much attention, though. They are always straying, pushing through holes in fences, taking advantage of gates left open, getting out, getting away, getting lost. One neighbor's goats, another neighbor's cows regularly invaded my garden until I made a big fuss and both guys fixed their fences. Dee's voluminous Vietnamese pigs liked to leave their pen and loll in the middle of the road, endlessly frustrating the FedEx deliveryman. A burro named Bravo dropped in for an overnight visit and was not entirely cooperative when his owner and her two little girls (who learned his whereabouts from our report to the sheriff's office) came to claim him. Strange dogs cruise through the place frequently, including an engaging pair of Great Pyrenees puppies and an enterprising beagle who ate the rattlesnake skull that Bill had parked on an ant nest so that the ants could clean off the flesh.

Texas is still the Wild West in some ways: you can shoot somebody who is threatening you or your property, and chances are good that the grand jury will refuse to indict. But let your animals wander and you can be liable for damages caused by their excursions. In Moby's case, however—well, as I say, I'm not sure the fence has been built that would keep him from indulging his lustful fancies, which is probably how he escaped in the first place. For the moment, we have to trust our barbwire and hope that Blossom keeps her head—or rather, her virginity. I tell Bill that I'm glad it's stopped raining (did my prayer help?) and that I hope he can flush soon.

"When did you say you were coming home?" he asks, although I'm sure he knows the plan.

"Next Saturday," I remind him. "Unless you need me sooner."

"No, I don't *need* you," he says, grumpy again. "I want you, that's all. Is that okay?"

I smile. "It's okay," I say.

THE RAIN STOPS early enough for me to get my binoculars and take a walk through the cool evening, down the oval road and around the eastern lawn of the Big House, where several does and their fawns are silently grazing across the luminescent grass. The sun is dropping to the west in a crystalline sky. To the east, a mauve sky displays a slender crescent moon. A great kiskadee, smartly masked in black and white, yellow belly as bright as new gold, flashes into a retama tree, where I can see the dim outline of a domed nest made of grass, bark, and twigs. The bird has a mouthful of dragonflies, and probably a nestful of young kiskadees. I pause, watching, and a few minutes later the bird is out again, shouting his name into the evening silence, *kis-ka-dee, kis-ka-deeee*, adding an incomprehensible footnote of raucous chatter. And then he's off to look for the last meal of the day, a lizard or a mouse or ripe fruit, a beetle, a small snake, a fish, if he can find one—anything to feed that brood.

Walking again, in the evening that has grown very quiet in the absence of the kiskadee, so still that the loudest sounds are the sibilant come-and-go of breath, the comforting thud of my heart. A few paces along, I glance down at my feet and see a click beetle, shiny black, like patent leather. This one is already dead (he's escaped the predation of the kiskadee) and I won't get to hear him click or see him jump: the cleverly athletic trick he's learned of somersaulting to his feet when he lands (as beetles often do) on his back. This one is an "eyed" click beetle, named for the large spectacle-like eyespots on top of his head, with a dark V under them that looks, for all the world, like Groucho Marx's moustache—patches of enameled coloring designed to make eager kiskadees and other predators think before they pounce. Since the beetle has no more use of his carcass, I pick it up.

And as if these gifts—the sight of the kiskadee, the beetle's carcass—aren't enough, I turn to see that the lavender sky to the east has darkened with birds, with billowing clouds of Mississippi kites, swooping and rising and turning and kettling, thousands and thousands of kites. And not just kites but hawks as well, Swainson's and Cooper's and sharp-shinned and broad-winged, migrating from their winter grounds to the south, heading north for breeding, stopping here to rest for the night. They are caught in the last luminous rays of the sun, so that they flash, fire, flame like rising and falling stars, like meteors against the darkening sky. I watch, awed, breathing the sight into my lungs, into my heart, into my blood as these raptors settle into the trees to the east, becoming the trees, until my arms ache from holding the binoculars and the last liquid light has darkened into night.

"Beautiful my desire," Theodore Roethke writes, "and the place of my desire."

It's enough. It's more than enough.

THE DAYS GO BY LIKE THIS, as I settle into a quiet pattern of worship, reading, meals, meditation, and knitting, which is for me a kind of meditation. I've made my own *altarcito*, decorated with gifts of this place: the orange oriole feather, the silver sprig of estafiate, the shiny black click beetle carcass, a mesquite twig covered with gray and orange lichen, a papery brown snakeskin. I do nothing for long, quiet spaces of time, thereby learning that doing nothing is much harder than doing something.

And I walk. I walk east around the Big House to the Kenedy cemetery, east to the sunrise and the trees where the migrating kites and hawks settled like fallen stars on that magical night. West to the cross at the crossroads, farther west to the sunset and the open pastures of coastal bluestem and cordgrass, still green in this springtime of rains. South to the Cowboy Cemetery and the tiny lake; north as far as I can go, to the boundaries of Lebh Shomea. And around and around the nature trails, through the thorny wilderness to islands of meditation called Gethsemane, Bethel, Zion. Like the raptors, I am a nomad, a visitor: I can't make a garden here, or leave any mark on this place, so I belong to it by making these daily rounds, watching for gifts, listening for messages, blessing and being blessed by all I see and touch and hear and smell.

In this way of belonging, I am not doing a new thing. On the Sunday before Ascension Day in pre-Reformation England, priest and parishioners—men, women, children—annually walked the borders of their parish, and farmers and small-holders walked the perimeters of their fields. For the religious, this was Rogationtide, a day to seek God's blessings on the fields and barns (the Latin *rogare* means to ask or to seek). For the secular, it was known as "beating the bounds," a ceremony in which the owner of a piece of property would tap each marker or landmark in turn with a willow or ash wand, acknowledging it as a sign of boundary, of ownership and responsibility, of the relationship between inner and outer, edge and interior, here and beyond.

Before maps, this ritualistic walkabout was a way of remembering limits and confirming landmarks, the hedges, trees, streams, ponds, and hills that were the signs, the icons of belonging. For mothers and fathers, it was a way to teach their children the circumference of the place within which most of them would live out their lives and to which they would be deeply, even tenderly attached—true landscapes of the heart. For farmers, it was a check on the boundaries of the fields, to make sure that no marker had been moved and no alien claim laid against the land. For all, it was a definition of self in a storied world, in place, bounded, located, landmarked, protected, enveloped, surrounded, known. It was a community's means of renewing and reconfirming its relationship to what Edward Relph calls "fields of care," places in which we share common experiences and to which we feel deeply, profoundly connected.

In this sense, the ritual of rogation established the participants as true caretakers, those who do not merely possess the land but are possessed *of* it: are members of its community, not just of humans, but of hills and valleys, soils, waters, weathers, plants, and animals. Other cultures practice this same kind of ritualized connection to the land. The Yamabushi, for instance, a Japanese Buddhist sect whose members made pilgrimage around their mountain in a counterclockwise direction related to the mandala that connected the earth and the cosmos in sacred space. Better known: the Australian aborigines who trek from one important landmark to another on their walkabouts, singing their world into life. "Aboriginal Creation myths," writes Bruce Chatwin in his famous book, *The Songlines*, "tell of the legendary totemic beings who had wandered over the continent in the Dreamtime, singing out the name of everything that crossed their path—birds, animals, plants, rocks, waterhold—and so singing the world into existence." Each singer, moreover, had a critical responsibility as a member of the community, for he or she inherited both a part of the song and the landscape to which the song belonged: none could rid themselves of the territory or of their obligation to preserve the song. The songlines were maps to actual territory, but more than that, to each individual's spiritual geography.

Through rituals like these, individuals become not just caretakers of the land, but also caretakers of the community's understanding of itself, and most especially of its stories, through which the sacred order of the land and its people are continued. For it is with story that our relationship to place is established, through story that we connect the interior and exterior landscapes, and in story that the individual person becomes, in Barry Lopez's words, "a reflection of the myriad enduring relationships of the landscape."

The seventeenth-century poet-priest George Herbert, observing that the old custom of rogation was in danger of dying out, advised his country parson to love and practice it for its four "manifest advantages":

> First, a blessing of God for the fruits of the field: Secondly, justice in the Preservation of bounds: Thirdly, Charity in loving walking, and neigh-bourly accompanying one another, with reconciling of differences at that time, if there be any: Fourthly, Mercy in releeving the poor by a liberall distribution and largesse . . . .

I remember this as I go on my walks, and think how dire is our need to practice this celebration of belonging to the land and to each other: invoking blessing, preserving the boundaries of our care, reconciling differences about those boundaries, and sharing what we have with those who have less—opening up the landscape of our hearts to any who would enter and contribute to the community's well-being. It might help our placeless culture to recollect and recover our sense of place, our responsibility to place, our stewardship for place, our devotion to place. It might help us to remember the difference between land-as-community and land-as-commodity and to ask ourselves what it means to designate some as "illegal aliens," to deny them the right to work and live on the land or parcel out that right in unjust ways. It might help us to understand that unless we respect the long-term needs of the land, we, too, are aliens here.

Naturalist Terry Tempest Williams has said that knowing our home places—belonging, being part of, being deeply accountable to our homes, our neighborhoods, our communities—is essential to caring for the land. We need to be "rooted deeply in place," she says, to make the commitment to "dig in and stay put." We need to learn our boundaries, our borders, and the names of the plants and animals with whom we co-inhabit a place. "If we don't know the names of things," she adds,

> if we don't know pronghorn antelope, if we don't know blacktail jack-rabbit, if we don't know sage, pinyon, juniper, then I think we are living a life without specificity, and then our lives become abstractions. Then we enter a place of true desolation. I remember a phone call from a friend of mine who lives along the MacKenzie River. She said, "This is the first year in twenty that the chinook salmon have not returned." This woman knows the names of things. This woman is committed to a place. And she sounded the alarm.

Sounding the alarm. We are all now under the threat of global climate change, and we should all be sounding the alarm as we observe the changes in our neighborhoods, our communities, our landscapes. Which means that we need to learn to know the names of things, understand the habits and habitats of plants, animals, birds. To be committed to a place means that we need to know every inch of the landscapes of our hearts.

This is something to think about here, in the Wild Horse Desert, where the savanna grasslands have been overtaken by a man-created wilderness of brush and thorn, and where this wilderness, in its turn, may be overtaken by the waters of the Gulf, when sea levels rise in an era of global warming. Where the Karankawa were evicted from their native place-communities, to be replaced by successions of Spanish, Mexican, and Texan landowners. Where although the land has been held by a single clan for a hundred and fifty years, its ownership is still open to challenge by those who claim a truer title.

All of which makes me wonder. If belonging to the land is an important part of being fully human, how are we to belong to land like this, which has belonged, over the centuries, to so many?

And what does it mean to "belong," anyway?

THE BIG WHITE CHAROLAIS BULL has gone home, Bill tells me. Moby's owner, a woman, came to claim him, towing a Moby-sized stock trailer so long that it wouldn't make the right-angle turn at our pasture gate. Coaxed with a bucket of his favorite cow cake into our cow pen and apparently accustomed to being fetched and toted, Moby trudged meekly up the ramp, allowed the gate to be fastened behind him, and was thence transported (presumably) home. When I ask Bill how he knew that Moby truly belonged to the woman who claimed him, he only laughs.

"Anybody with the guts to haul that bull can have him, as far as I'm concerned," he says. "Anyway, possession is nine-tenths of the law. She has him now. He's her problem."

And Blossom? Since the fence is intact, we're guessing that she is, too.

Maybe Moby's lust was mainly a matter of imagination, his or hers.

Or ours.

ON FRIDAY EVENING, just at sunset, I climb once again to the tower on the top of *La Casa Grande*, still thinking about land as commodity, land as community, land and change. It's easy to see the visible signs of community here within the boundaries of Lebh Shomea, a fellowship of those who come to lose and find themselves in the silence of the Sacred, in a landscape cared for by those who define this as a sacred place and accept their responsibility to it as a sacred obligation. A change from the ranch, yes, and in most ways very different. But somehow I think that Mifflin and Petra Kenedy, Quaker and Catholic, would understand the mission of this community and respect its use of the land.

I can see a different kind of community if I turn in another direction, toward that vast green ebb and flow of wilderness rippling east to the Gulf and far to the south: an interdependent community of soils and plants and birds and mammals and reptiles, existing for its own sake and to the virtual exclusion of humans, who cannot make their way through this natural sanctuary.

It is sadly true, though, that this stinging, singing, shimmering world of thorn and thicket is the product of man-made change. It sprang from the ignorant carelessness of the first European colonists who introduced two potentially destructive domesticated animals—cattle and horses—and failed to control their range or their numbers. And it grew from the greed of ranchers who saw the land as their commodity to exploit. Like the stockmen's association in West Texas, around the turn of the twentieth century, which declared, in no uncertain terms:

> Resolved that none of us know, or care to know, anything about grasses, native or otherwise, outside of the fact that for the present, there are lots

of them, the best on record, and we are after getting the most of them while they last.

They did get the most of them, too. And those rich West Texas grasses didn't last any longer than the native grasses here in the Wild Horse Desert or the oil under the ground in both places. The grass is gone and oil production peaked in the state, in the United States, in the 1970s—the oil that spouted out in such abundance that its early discoverers could imagine no bottom to the barrel. The thorns have inherited the earth—at least here, and at least for now, until the polar ice sheets melt and the oceans rise and the waters of the Gulf once more drown these coastal plains.

Global warming, created in large part by humans' burning of fossil fuels, is caused by the same blithe disregard for the consequences that allowed those West Texas ranchers to vow to use up all the grass just as fast as they could. The grasses on the land, the oil under the land—it's all part of the same pattern. It's here, it's ours, let's use it, let's use it up.

But Sarita Kenedy is said to have hated the oil business and wanted nothing to do with it, believing that the grasslands—wisely maintained, carefully used—were made for cows, not oil rigs. The drilling rigs, the pumps, the pipelines—they seemed to her to be ugly invaders, destroying the peace of the land, its quiet, the solitude of cows and calves and vaqueros, and she did her best to ignore these changes as they came. It is also true that she did her best, in her last few years, to turn land-as-commodity into land-as-community by rewriting her will so that the land would not go to individuals, for their private use, but to an organization that would turn the land and its products to good for needy people beyond the borders of the land. As Herbert says, "Mercy in releeving the poor by a liberall distribution and largesse."

The sun is setting to the west, and all the green land, this wilderness of thorn and thicket and grass and sea, settling into the stillness of twilight, is bathed in a soft amber glow. A nighthawk, expert bug catcher, darts and zigzags, turning on the tip of a wing in the empty air while purple martins glide in wide, sliding circles, circumscribing their own sweep of sky. Somewhere not far away, a horse whinnies, a dog barks. A great horned owl speaks his nocturnal mind, celebrating the coming darkness, and another answers with a tender *who-who-whoo*. As the full moon rises up out of the Gulf, a single coyote yips joyfully, alone in the ancient flooding moonlight, at home in the wholeness of the world, feeling herself free, free and infinite, coyote self extending beyond the boundaries of skin into the vastness of earth and moon and stars. She is joined by another and another and another in a primitive chorus of delirious ecstasy, claiming the night and the Wild Horse Desert.

I sit quietly, watching, listening to the owls, to the coyotes, to the desert, to my breath, as dark falls, silently, silently. All this, all this, all. And all precious beyond words.

And then, with a full heart, I walk back to Ezekiel for a night of silent rest. Tomorrow I go home.

CHAPTER EIGHTEEN

In Place and Free

One who returns home—to one's marriage and household and place in the world—desiring anew what was previously chosen, is neither the world's stranger nor its prisoner, but is at once in place and free.

WENDELL BERRY, *THE UNSETTLING OF AMERICA*

THERE'S NOTHING VERY SPECIAL about Meadow Knoll, not really, except that we have lived in this place for more than twenty years, long enough to know the fragile grasses and the animals who live among them, the sturdy trees and their birds, the creek and its dwellers, the now-and-then moods of the changeable sky, the slant of the sun against the blessing of the hills.

But that is enough. For me, that is everything, and as I drive through the gate and down the lane, I think with pleasure and a sense of relief, yes, I am home. And then, so quickly that it is not a second thought, but a stumbling into the real meaning of the first: no, *I am* home. Home is where I am. And that is right, and good, and true.

Things have changed in my absence—they always do, in small ways and large—and I notice the changes as I drive down the road on the other side of the lake. The culvert was seriously washed out by the rains, and Boggy Junction was a muddy mess—looks like the garbage truck got stuck there again. The nomad who owns the junkyard hauled several more wrecked cars onto the place, and the ugly detritus of human progress was visible from the road. He began building a fence last year to screen the view, but setting posts was as far as he got. Too much work, maybe. Not enough money, not enough care. Another nomad installed a second trailer on his lot—although maybe he's just trading up, and the old one will be hauled away. The woman who lives in the trailer above the lake dumped a second discarded refrigerator into the hole she dug beside the road. The land, empty when we came here, is filling up with humans and their junk, and there's no gain in loveliness. When I'm away, I forget these scars, these evidences of human misuse. Coming home to them is no pleasure.

But farther along, on our private lane, the landscape is unscarred. With the recent rains, Bill hasn't been able to mow; the grasses are thigh-high, brightened by sunflowers and daisy fleabane and the first bright flickers of fall goldenrod. Grasshoppers fly up beside the car, a rabbit darts in front of me, a cardinal, red as a fiery ember, alights in a green cedar. As I stop the car, I see that the climbing roses are blooming pink and white, the salvia is a mound of brilliant indigo spikes, and the artemisia spills silver along the walk. I greet the sweetly familiar land with something akin to the coyotes' primitive ecstasy, but more restrained. I don't howl.

The dogs rush out to greet me, gleefully barking, bouncing and licking and pawing, happy that I am home and that their pack is once again complete. Bill follows, offering a welcoming embrace and a kiss meant to erase time apart and distance. But time cannot always be canceled with a kiss. There are places in me where he cannot go, and places in him where I am not invited. It will take days to adjust to being together, to refit our separate selves into the comfortable patterns we have learned, to forget (if we can) whatever fears and resentments and rejections we conjured up while we were apart.

Can we? *Can we?* There's always that question and never an answer. What I cherish about this home and this marriage are their securities, their reliable bulwarks against encroaching change, but I know that this is only an illusion. However much I might wish it otherwise, home is no fortress against time and change and death. And marriage, even when it is healthy and loving, is also fragile, and no defense against fear and loss.

Still, it's what I have, what Bill and I have together. And I think again, yes, I am home, and then: no, *we* are home. Home is where *we* are. And that is right, too, at least for now.

I unpack and put things away and then we walk with the dogs along the length of the creek, past Turtle Pool and into Lazarus' Meadow. The old mesquite is finally gone, transformed into bowls and graceful vases, but Bill shows me the pecans on the trees, a big crop this year, heavy enough to weigh down the limber branches. A hawk lifts powerfully into the bluest of blue skies. A squirrel chatters (these are his pecans, too, and he wants us to take note of the fact). A monarch butterfly, bright nomad, dances on the tips of grass.

All of us—Bill and I, the hawk, the squirrel, the butterfly—are beating our bounds, tracing our trajectories, learning where we are, in a ritual walkabout that brings each of us home again. For me, the pools and banks and trees and plants, the hawk, the squirrel, the monarch are the signs, the icons of my belonging to this place. Through them, I am defined in the world, bounded and located, landmarked. "I walk in the world to love it," Mary Oliver has said. I walk in this place to love it, and to be loved by it and in it, for as long as life and death and change allow.

And later, after soup and sandwiches and a quiet evening, lying in bed with the window open and the room flooded with the moon's silver brightness, I hear a coyote singing, her coyote self filled with the infinity of night and stars, at home in the wholeness, loving the loveliness of the world, in place and free.

NOTES

PROLOGUE. DOCUMENTING A LIFE

p. ix. *It is our inward journey. One Writer's Beginnings*, by Eudora Welty (New York: Warner Books, 1991), p. 112.

CHAPTER ONE. MEADOW KNOLL: GETTING HERE, ALONE TOGETHER

p. 6. *This was "work for hire."* When a writer does this kind of work, he or she relinquishes all rights to the work, which is assigned by an editor and written to the editor's specifications. The work is usually published under a pseudonym, and the publisher owns the copyright. Many writers don't like to work this way because it is an anonymous kind of writing.

p. 10. *a people of highways.* "Locating America," by Wayne Fields, in *The Idea of Place*, by Milica Banjanin, et al. (St. Louis, Mo.: Washington University, University College Occasional Papers, 2, Winter 1982–1983), pp. 18–20.

p. 11. *exile is in our time.* "Roots," by John Berryman, in *Henry's Fate & Other Poems 1967– 1972* (New York: Farrar, Straus and Giroux, 1977), p. 58.

p. 11. *a new kind of wanting.* Some ten years after this experience, I came across the book *Place and Placelessness*, by Edward Relph (London: Pion, 1976). Relph helped me put a name to what I had felt and gave me a useful conceptual framework within which to describe the place-experiences of my childhood and early adult years. His definitions of "insideness" and "outsideness" allowed me to see my shifts in place-understanding in broader cultural terms.

CHAPTER TWO. WHERE IN THE WORLD

p. 14. *If we are to live responsibly. Writing from the Center*, by Scott Russell Sanders (Bloomington: Indiana University Press, 1997), pp. 20–21.

p. 16. *institutional fault line. The Great Plains*, by Walter Prescott Webb (Lincoln: University of Nebraska Press, 1981).

p. 16. *The thin soil is calcareous.* As a non-geologist, I have been helped by *Roadside Geology of Texas*, by Darwin Spearing (Missoula, Mont.: Mountain Press, 1991). Two other books for non-scientists on my bookshelf: *A Field Guide to Fossils of Texas*, by Charles Finsley (Houston: Gulf Publishing Company, 1999), and *Lone Star Dinosaurs*, by Louis L. Jacobs (College Station: Texas A&M University Press, 1999.)

p. 17. *Neighboring Llano County.* These historical rainfall data were provided to me by Bob Rose, meteorologist, Lower Colorado River Authority, Austin, Texas.

p. 19. *This fortunate location.* On the Balcones Canyonlands and the Lampasas Cut Plain as ecological regions, see *Birds & Other Wildlife of South Central Texas,* by Edward A. Kutac and S. Christopher Caran (Austin: University of Texas Press, 1994), pp. 8–11.

p. 19. *We also have several Texas redbuds.* My favorite reference work for trees: *Trees of Central Texas,* by Robert A. Vines (Austin: University of Texas Press, 1984).

p. 19. *two solitudes. Letters to a Young Poet,* by Rainer Maria Rilke (New York: W. W. Norton and Co., 1962), Letter 7.

p. 21. *native to this place. Native to This Place,* by Wes Jackson (New York: Counterpoint Press, 1996).

CHAPTER THREE. MOVING THROUGH, MOVING ON, MOVING IN

p. 22. *I read the landscape. From Where We Stand: Recovering a Sense of Place,* by Deborah Tall (Baltimore: Johns Hopkins University Press, 1996), p. 25.

p. 25. *I imagine the Tonkawas.* This and my other remarks about the prehistoric peoples of Texas are based on W. W. Newcomb Jr.'s book, *The Indians of Texas From Prehistoric to Modern Times* (Austin: University of Texas Press, 1961). On prehistoric peoples, pp. 3–25; on the Tonkawas, pp. 133–153; on the Comanches, 153–191.

p. 26. *And while I'm thinking of violent scenes.* The story of the Johnson ambush is told in *Indian Depredations in Texas,* by J. W. Wilbarger (Austin, 1889, facsimile reprint Abilene, Tex: McWhiney Foundation Press, 1991), and in the obituary of one of the surviving Johnson children, published in the Florence, Texas, *Vidette,* Thursday, April 3, 1924, and reprinted in *The Sun,* Georgetown, Texas, June 28, 1973. Wilbarger details fifteen instances of battles, ambushes, and murders that took place in Burnet County during the 1860s and 1870s.

p. 27. *But farmers on this "prodigal frontier."* On the "prodigal frontier" and its aftermath in Somervell County in north central Texas, see *Hard Scrabble: Observations on a Patch of Land,* by John Graves (Houston: Gulf Publishing Company, 1973). Also, *Harder than Hardscrabble: Oral Recollections of the Farming Life from the Edge of the Texas Hill Country,* edited by Thad Sitton (Austin: University of Texas Press, 2003). This collection of oral histories comes from an area just forty miles to the north of us, now the site of the U.S. Army's Fort Hood.

p. 28. *A friend from Houston once told me. Places in the World a Person Could Walk,* by David Syring (Austin: University of Texas Press, 2000), p. 9.

CHAPTER FOUR. DWELLING, ROOTING, LEARNING

p. 31. *As much as we live in a place. Stepping Westward: The Long Search for Home in the Pacific Northwest,* by Sallie Tisdale (New York: Perennial, 1993), p. 9.

p. 31. *Home is where. A Voice in the Wilderness: Conversations with Terry Tempest Williams,* edited by Michael Austin (Logan: Utah State University Press, 2006), p. 52.

p. 35. *Nothing can grow. The Autobiography,* by William Carlos Williams (New York: New Directions, 1951), p. 334.

p. 35. *If they have any awareness of place.* On the highways along which we commute: Relph

(p. 52) calls this "incidental outsideness," a situation in which place is the background or setting, such as the neighborhoods and spaces through which we drive on our way somewhere else.

p. 36. *but they have no authentic sense of place.* According to Relph (p. 64), an authentic sense of place is a "direct and genuine experience of the entire complex of the identity of places, not mediated and distorted through a series of quite arbitrary social and intellectual fashions about how that experience should be, nor following stereotyped conventions."

p. 40. *Every American Indian tribe.* See *Native American Ethnobotany*, by Daniel Moerman (Portland, Ore.: Timber Press, 1998), p. 118.

p. 42. *Learning that goldenrod sap contained.* See *Legends & Lore of Texas Wildflowers*, by Elizabeth Silverthorne (College Station: Texas A&M University Press, 1996), p. 62.

p. 42. *And with each gust.* A *Sand County Almanac*, by Aldo Leopold (New York: Ballantine Books 1970), p. 8.

p. 43. *Less than 1 percent remains.* The Native Texas Prairies Association, www.texasprairie. org, accessed August 5, 2007. For more about Texas prairies, see *Prairie Time: A Blackland Portrait*, by Matt White (College Station: Texas A&M University Press, 2006); *Grasses of the Texas Hill Country: A Field Guide*, by Brian Loflin and Shirley Loflin (College Station: Texas A&M University Press, 2006); and *Wildflowers of Texas*, by Geyata Ajilvsgi (Bryan, Tex.: Shearer Publishing, 1998).

p. 43. *We came with visions.* The *Gift of Good Land: Further Essays Cultural and Agricultural*, by Wendell Berry (New York: North Point Press, 1981), p. 82.

CHAPTER FIVE. NAMING

p. 46. *The naming calls.* Poetry, Language, Thought, by Martin Heidegger (New York: Harper & Row, 1971), p. 196.

p. 46. *To hear the unembodied call of a place.* "Introduction," by Barry Lopez, in *Home Ground: Language for an American Landscape*, edited by Barry Lopez (San Antonio: Trinity University Press, 2006), p. xviii.

p. 48. *We need a richer vocabulary of place.* Writing *From the Center*, by Scott Russell Sanders (Bloomington: Indiana University Press, 1997), p. 18.

p. 48. *As Barry Lopez remarks.* In *Home Ground*, Lopez describes two maps of a section of the Susitna Valley in Alaska. "The map on the left bristled with more than a hundred colored pushpins, each bearing a tiny paper flag with a Deni'ina place-name on it, the Athabaskan language spoken by the indigenous people still living there. Fewer than a dozen names appeared in English on the [map on the] right . . ." (p. xv).

p. 55. *An "I-You" relationship with place.* In Relph, p. 78.

CHAPTER SIX. ALL OUR FOOD IS SOULS

p. 56. *If you are what you eat.* Attributed to Claude Fischler, nutritional sociologist with the French National Center for Scientific Research.

p. 58. *In 1985, I read. Diet for a Small Planet*, by Frances Moore Lappé (New York: Ballantine, 1985); *Laurel's Kitchen*, by Laurel Robertson (Berkeley, Calif.: Nilgiri Press, 1978).

p. 64. *Good efforts, I think. Animal, Vegetable, Miracle: A Year of Food Life*, by Barbara Kingsolver (New York: HarperCollins, 2007); *The Omnivore's Dilemma: A Natural History of Four Meals*, by Michael Pollan (New York: Penguin Press, 2006).

CHAPTER SEVEN. GAINING, LOSING

p. 69. *Things as they are.* "The Sacred and the Lost," by Norman Fischer, in *Inquiring Mind* 14 (1997), No. 1, p. 5.

p. 74. *By June our brook's run out of song.* "Hyla Brook," by Robert Frost from *Mountain Interval* (New York: Henry Holt and Company, 1920).

CHAPTER EIGHT. RIGHT LIVELIHOOD

p. 75. *I am a competent but essentially invisible writer. The Writing Trade: A Year in the Life*, by John Jerome (New York: Lyons & Burford, 1992), p. 3.

p. 77. *Bill called us the "book-a-month club."* A full bibliography is available on our Web site, www.mysterypartners.com.

p. 79. *the "useful plants."* The Herb Society of America offers a broad definition of an herb: it is a plant "for use and delight." Herbs include medicinal, culinary, fiber, dye, and crafting plants.

p. 81. *But modern writers. Shameless Promotion for Brazen Hussies II: Practical Publicity Tips*, compiled by Gay Toltl Kinman and Claire McNab, published by Sisters in Crime, and available through www.sistersincrime.org.

CHAPTER NINE. ALONE, TOGETHER, APART

p. 84. *I hold this to be. Letters to a Young Poet*, by Rainer Maria Rilke (New York: W. W. Norton and Co., 1962), Letter 4.

p. 87. *And when we are constantly with other people.* On the persona, see *The Collected Works*, Vol. 6, by C. G. Jung, translated by R. C. F. Hull, Bollingen Series XX (Princeton: Princeton University Press), especially Chapter 11, pp. 463–470.

p. 88. *Our job is to find ourselves.* The sacred within is an important concept in Eastern spirituality: "Do not be led by reports, or tradition, or hearsay. Be not led by the authority of religious texts, nor by mere logic or inference, nor by considering appearances, nor by the delight in speculative opinions, nor by seeming possibilities, nor by the idea: 'this is our teacher.' But O Kalamas, when you know for yourselves that certain things are unwholesome and wrong, and bad, then give them up. . . . And when you know for yourselves that certain things are wholesome and good, then accept them and follow them." From the *Anguttara-nikaya*, quoted in *What the Buddha Taught*, by Walpola Rahula (New York: Grove Press, 1974), p. 3.

p. 88. *A moment of recognition. A Gradual Awakening,* by Stephen Levine (New York: Anchor/Doubleday, 1979), p. 45.

p. 89. *The moment of awakening. Zen Keys,* by Thich Nhat Hanh (Garden City: Anchor/Doubleday, 1974), p. 41.

p. 91. *The monastery is … a place. A Listening Heart: The Spirituality of Sacred Sensuousness,* by David Steindl-Rast (New York: Crossroad Publishing, 1992), p. 17.

CHAPTER TEN. LEBH SHOMEA: GETTING HERE, ALONE

p. 94. *nine miles of paved roads.* Texas Association of Counties, County Information Project, www.county.org/resources/countydata/index.asp, accessed January 10, 2007.

p. 95. *The road is valuable.* "Opening a Road," *Time,* December 30, 1940.

p. 96. *Guests who share.* The community's Web site is www.lebhshomea.org.

p. 96. *Silence is God's first language. Foundations for Centering Prayer and the Christian Contemplative Life,* by Thomas Keating (New York: Continuum International Publishing Group, 2002), p. 203.

p. 100. *to try to love the questions. Letters to a Young Poet,* by Rainer Maria Rilke (New York: W. W. Norton and Co., 1962), Letter 4.

p. 103. *inner psycho-topography of all humans. Landscapes of the Sacred: Geography and Narrative in American Spirituality,* by Belden C. Lane (New York: Paulist Press, 1988), p. 79.

CHAPTER ELEVEN. SILENCE

p. 104. *There is nothing in all the universe. Meister Eckhart,* by Meister Eckhart (New York: HarperOne, 1957), p. 244.1

p. 107. *what was available at the time.* On our reading list: *Solitude: A Return to the Self,* by Anthony Storr (New York: Ballantine Books, 1989); *Peace is Every Step: The Path of Mindfulness in Everyday Life,* by Thich Nhat Hanh (New York: Bantam Books, 1992); *The Heart of Stillness: The Elements of Spiritual Discipline,* by David A. Cooper (New York: Bell Tower/Crown, 1992); and *Monastery Without Walls,* by Bruce Davis (Berkeley, Calif.: Celestial Arts, 1990).

p. 107. *borrowing a term from Eastern mystics.* The concept of the Witness is found throughout many ancient texts. From the Advaitin classic, the *Yoga Vasistha:* "You [the Self] dwell in me in a state of equilibrium as pure witness consciousness, without form and without the divisions of time and space." Clarifying and strengthening witnessing awareness is the chief focus of Buddhist meditation.

CHAPTER TWELVE. SEEING THROUGH TIME

p. 111. *All inhabited landscapes.* Tall, p. 24.

p. 111. *To be human is to live.* Relph, p. 1.

p. 113. *One must strip the fruit. The La Salle Expedition to Texas: The Journal of Henri Joutel, 1684–1687*, edited by William C. Foster (Austin: Texas State Historical Association, 1998), p. 114.

p. 114. *Nobody would be surprised.* For a detailed report on the claim, see "Sarita's Secret," by Gary Cartwright, *Texas Monthly Magazine*, September 2004.

p. 115. *Still, on sweltering July and August days.* As I was writing this, Father Kelly Nemeck told me that all of the dwellings were recently air-conditioned, as well as both chapels and a few of the rooms in the Big House. "For the vast majority of the people who come here," he said, "air-conditioning is no longer a convenience but a necessity. Such are the times in which we live. Some call it progress."

p. 116. *When she was a little drunk. If You Love Me You Will Do My Will*, by Stephen G. Michaud and Hugh Aynesworth (New York: Signet, 1991), p. xix.

p. 119. *This early culture was followed.* On the Aransas group and the Karankawas, see "Prehistoric and Early Historic People and Environment in the Corpus Christi Bay Area," by Robert A. Ricklis, in the Publications Library of the Coastal Bend and Estuaries Program, www.cbbep.org/publications/virtuallibrary/ricklis.html, accessed August 7, 2007.

p. 119. *The success of these people was compounded.* Newcomb, p. 56.

p. 120. A translation of de Vaca's astonishing account is available online: www.pbs.org/weta/thewest/resources/archives/one/cabeza.htm, accessed September 14, 2008.

p. 120. *They do the same thing with the priests.* Newcomb, pp. 77–78. De Solis was writing in 1767–1768.

p. 121. *There arises from their bodies.* Newcomb, p. 67.

p. 122. *The Karánkaways are gone. Karankaway Country*, by Roy Bedichek (Austin: University of Texas Press, 1950), p. 16.

CHAPTER THIRTEEN. SPIRITS OF THE PLACE: *EL DESIERTO DE LOS MUERTOS*

p. 123. *I sit in the cool back room. The True Solitude: Selections from the Writings of Thomas Merton*, by Thomas Merton (Kansas City, Mo.: Hallmark Editions, 1969), pp. 58–59.

p. 123. *And places themselves.* Relph, p. 33.

p. 127. *There is a way of beholding nature. The Moon by Whale Light*, by Diane Ackerman (New York: Random House, 1991), p. xiv.

p. 129. *He did his part for the cause.* On the importance of Civil War Bagdad, see *Boom and Bust: The Historical Cycles of Matamoros and Brownsville*, by Milo Kearney and Anthony Knopp (Austin, Texas: Eakin Press, 1991).

p. 129. *It took a peculiar kind of alchemy.* On Kenedy, King, and cotton during the Civil War, see *The Kings of Texas: The 150-Year Saga of an American Ranching Empire*, by Don Graham (Hoboken, N.J.: John Wiley and Son, 2003), pp. 96–105.

p. 130. *In many ways.* For the vaqueros' stories, read *Voices from the Wild Horse Desert: The Vaquero Families of the King and Kenedy Ranches*, by Jane Clements Monday and Betty Bailey Colley (Austin: University of Texas Press, 1997).

p. 130. *How did Isaac find his way here?* According to Father Kelly, Isaac Hodges was almost certainly black. His daughter, Elizabeth Hodges, served as nanny to Sarita and Johnny. The Kenedy Ranch is reported to have employed several black vaqueros, who were outstanding cowboys.

p. 130. *And without the women.* See the chapter titled "The Vaquero Family," Monday and Colley, pp. 118–160.

p. 130. *La Parra wasn't the first.* The most recent and reliable biographical information about Mifflin Kenedy appears in *Petra's Legacy: The South Texas Ranching Empire of Petra Vela and Mifflin Kenedy,* by Jane Clements Monday and Frances Brannen Vick (College Station: Texas A&M University Press, 2007).

p. 132. *by the time Texas joined the Confederacy.* For Kenedy's role in the war and the reconstruction of Brownville, see Monday and Vick, pp. 79–140.

p. 132. *more than one hundred men.* Monday and Vick, p. 57.

p. 133. *By 1875, things had gotten to such a desperate pass.* To taste the wildness of these outlaw times, read the memoir *Taming the Nueces Strip: The Story of McNelly's Rangers,* by George Durham and Clyde Wantland (Austin: University of Texas Press, 1982).

CHAPTER FOURTEEN. PLAINS FARE

p. 134. *Eating is an agricultural act.* Pollan, p. 11.

p. 134. *To pay attention.* "Yes! No!" by Mary Oliver from *White Pine: Poems and Prose Poems* (Boston: Beacon Press, 2006), p. 27.

p. 136. *We eat mindlessly. The Miracle of Mindfulness: A Manual on Meditation,* by Thich Nhat Hanh (Boston: Beacon Press, 1999), p. 5.

p. 137. V'achalta v'savata u'vayrachta. Deut. 8:10.

p. 138. *As Michael Pollan points out.* Pollan, p. 84.

p. 138. *I feel like a sick heifer.* Michaud and Aynesworth, p. xx.

p. 138. *Nilgaı are exotic game.* Price and game availability data come from the Web site of La Mansion de Sarita, Inc., www.lamansion.net*www.lamansion.net*, accessed August 9, 2007.

p. 139. *More recently, a prominent Texas food historian.* See *Dishes from the Wild Horse Desert: Norteño Cooking of South Texas,* by Melissa Guerra (Hoboken, N.J.: John Wiley & Sons, 2006), p. xii. And on the back jacket: "The Wild Horse Desert provided very little for the people that roamed and settled this harsh, hot land."

p. 140. *Mifflin Kenedy's Mexican wife.* The date of 1854 for their marriage is two years later than the one commonly accepted. See Michaud and Aynesworth, p. 229.

p. 141. *In frontier America. The Story of Corn,* by Betty Fussell (New York: Knopf, 1992), p. 220.

p. 141. *If Europeans held the New World corn in a lower regard.* For more on the early colonial conflict between the Mexican use of corn and the European preference for wheat, as well as other important cultural food differences, see *¡Que Vivan Los Tamales!: Food and the Making of Mexican Identity,* by Jeffrey M. Pilcher (Albuquerque: University of New Mexico Press, 1998).

p. 143. *We think of monks. Dakota: A Spiritual Geography*, by Kathleen Norris (Boston/New York: Houghton Mifflin Company, 1993), p. 191.

CHAPTER SIXTEEN. THE KENEDY WOMEN

p. 150. *Was Petra Vela Kenedy.* "Petra Vela and the Kenedy Family Legacy," by Ana Carolina Castillo Crimm, in *Tejano Epic: Essays in Honor of Félix D. Almaráz, Jr.*, edited by Arnoldo De León (Austin: Texas State Historical Association, 2005), p. 44.

p. 152. *Everything that grows.* Richard Harding Davis (1892), quoted in Graham, p. 195. Graham offers a thoroughly readable history of the challenges of ranching in the Nueces Strip. For a first-person account by one of the Texas Rangers assigned to bring peace to the lawless Strip, read *Taming the Nueces Strip: The Story of McNelly's Rangers*, by George Durham as told to Clyde Wantland.

p. 152. *There are two versions.* For a view of Petra as the daughter of a Mexican aristocrat, see *Las Tejanas: 300 Years of History*, by Teresa Palomo Acosta (Austin: University of Texas Press, 2003), pp. 49–51. For Petra as a "humble ranch girl," see Crimm, pp. 43–57. For a more complete and complex view of the strong, attractive woman who became the matriarch of one of the most important families in Texas history, see Monday and Vick, from which I have drawn most of this account.

p. 153. *Spanish mantilla of black lace.* Quoted in Crimm, p. 55.

p. 153. *the Kenedys had a house in Brownsville.* See "Storybook Mansions," by Murphy Givens, in *Corpus-Christi Caller*, Wednesday, June 27, 2001.

p. 155. *I think of two landscapes. Crossing Open Ground*, by Barry Lopez (New York: Vintage Books, 1989), pp. 64–65.

p. 156. *If there were any storms in Stella's placid life.* For the details of the Fernandez lawsuit and the alleged Kenedy paternity, see *Texas Monthly*, September 2004. The article can be read online at http://www.texasmonthly.com/2004-09-01/feature5php. The full text of the filings before the Texas Supreme Court may be found online at www.supreme.courts.state.tx.us/ebriefs/04/04060702.pdf, accessed January 23, 2007.

p. 156. *Of course, taking a mistress.* See "Seed of the Nation: Men's Sex and Potency in Mexico," by Matthew C. Gutmann, in *The Gender/Sexuality Reader: Culture, History, Political Economy*, edited by Roger N. Lancaster and Micaela di Leonardo (New York: Routledge, 1997), pp. 196–197.

p. 157. *Sarita East went on the range.* Quoted in Monday and Colley, p. 29.

p. 157. *The ladies got linens.* Quoted in Monday and Colley, p. 141.

p. 157. *A nephew described her as a "cowgirl."* See Michaud and Aynesworth, p. 47.

p. 157. *If somebody had a problem.* Quoted in Monday and Colley, p. 12.

p. 158. *obviously in love with him.* Quoted in Michaud and Aynesworth, p. 68; *our special relationship*, Michaud and Aynesworth, p. xxiv.

p. 159. *La Parra, she thought.* Michaud and Aynesworth, p. 70.

p. 159. *a daughter born out of wedlock.* Personal communication from Father Kelly Nemeck, based on his study of Carmen Morell Kenedy.

p. 159. *At its core.* "Cattle Barons of Texas Yore Accused of Epic Land Grab," by Sam Howe Verhovek, *New York Times*, July 14, 1997.

CHAPTER SEVENTEEN. BELONGING TO THE COMMUNITY OF THE LAND

p. 161. *We can change places.* Quoted (and translated from the French) in Relph, p. 41.

p. 161. *We abuse land because.* *A Sand County Almanac*, by Aldo Leopold (New York: Ballantine Books, 1970), pp. xviii–xix.

p. 165. *Beautiful my desire.* "The Rose," by Theodore Roethke in *The Far Field: Last Poems* (New York: Anchor Books, Doubleday, 1971), p. 31.

p. 166. *what Edward Relph calls "fields of care."* Settings in which we have had a multiplicity of experiences and which call forth an entire complex of affections and responses." Relph, pp. 38–39.

p. 166. *In this sense, the ritual.* See *LifePlace: Bioregional Thought and Practice*, by Robert L. Thayer Jr. (Berkeley: University of California Press, 2003), pp. 72–73. Thayer describes his own similar practice, helping his neighbors "re-enchant their watershed" by conducting a ritualized, clockwise tour of two local creeks.

p. 167. *Aboriginal Creation myths.* *The Songlines*, by Bruce Chatwin (New York: Penguin, 1987), p. 2.

p. 167. *a reflection of the myriad.* Lopez, *Crossing Open Ground*, p. 67.

p. 167. *First, a blessing of God.* *A Priest to the Temple or The Country Parson, His Character and Rule of Holy Life*, by George Herbert (Norwich: Canterbury Press, 2003), p. 83.

p. 168. *"If we don't know the names.* Austin, pp. 52–53.

p. 169. *Resolved that none of us know.* The Edwards County stockmen's association, 1898, quoted in *Miles from Nowhere: Tales from America's Contemporary Frontier*, by Dayton Duncan (New York: Penguin Books, 1994), pg. 145.

p. 170. *Sarita Kenedy is said to have hated.* See Michaud and Aynesworth, p. xxii.

CHAPTER EIGHTEEN. IN PLACE AND FREE

p. 172. *One who returns home.* *The Unsettling of America: Culture and Agriculture*, by Wendell Berry (San Francisco: Sierra Club Books, 1986), pp. 130–131.

p. 174. *I walk in the world.* *Long Life: Essays and Other Writings*, by Mary Oliver (Cambridge, Mass.: Da Capo Press, 2004), p. 40.